# Southern Homecoming Traditions

*Recipes and Remembrances*

## Carolyn Quick Tillery

CITADEL PRESS
Kensington Publishing Corp.
www.kensingtonbooks.com

CITADEL PRESS BOOKS are published by
Kensington Publishing Corp.
119 West 40th Street
New York, NY 10018



This is an abridged version of the hardcover edition of *Southern Homecoming Traditions*. It has been completely reset for this trade paperback edition.

All Kensington titles, imprints, and distributed lines are available at special quantity discounts for bulk purchases for sales promotions, premiums, fund-raising, educational, or institutional use. Special book excerpts or customized printings can also be created to fit specific needs. For details, write or phone the office of the Kensington special sales manager: Kensington Publishing Corp., 119 West 40th Street, New York, NY 10018, attn: Special Sales Department; phone 1-800-221-2647.



First hardcover printing: November 2006
First trade paperback printing: June 2010

10 9 8 7 6 5 4 3 2 1

Printed in the United States of America

Library of Congress Control Number: 2006929663

ISBN-13: 978-0-8065-3204-2
ISBN-10: 0-8065-3204-1

In loving memory of my beloved Margaret "Marwny" Wolf.

*As always, I first give all honor to God*
*and Jesus Christ, my Lord and Savior,*
*who goes before me as my Jehovah Nissi*
*or "Banner of Victory" and comes behind*
*as my strong rear guard!*

# Contents

# Preface: Atlanta and the Civil War

*"A House divided against itself cannot stand. I believe this government cannot endure permanently half slave and half free. I do not expect the Union to be dissolved—I do not expect the house to fall—but I do expect it will cease to be divided."*

**—Abraham Lincoln, U.S. Senate nomination acceptance speech, Springfield, Illinois, June 16, 1858**

ON JANUARY 19, 1861, Georgia seceded from the Union, declaring itself to be "a free and independent State." And by the time of the Civil War the city of Atlanta was a major Southern arsenal and rail terminus, making it a primary war target of the federal government. Because of its importance to the Confederate war effort, General Ulysses S. Grant ordered General William Tecumseh Sherman to "[inflict] all the damage you can against their war resources." Those resources were many and varied because Atlanta was prospering as a war supplier of the South, manufacturing railroad cars, revolvers, cannon, knives, saddles, spurs, buttons, belt buckles, tents, and canteens.

Total annihilation of this Southern war machine would be the hard-won trophy Sherman presented to Lincoln, virtually guaranteeing Lincoln's reelection. It also served as the key to Lincoln's "divide and conquer" strategy.

The Battle of Atlanta, on July 22, 1864, nearly destroyed the city; more than 10,000 people perished. Almost four months after seizing the city, Sherman ordered it burned and federal troops left only 400 of almost 4,000 buildings standing. The next day Sherman began his "march to the sea." Cutting himself off from Union supply lines, he intended to live off the land and proceeded to cut a swath of death and destruction 300 miles in length and 60 miles wide through Georgia, destroying factories, bridges, railroads, and public buildings. Pursuing a strategy of total war, Union troops not only broke the will of the people to fight, but also deprived them of any resources with which to attack. The Mayor of Atlanta led a city delegation to the corner of Marietta and Northside Drive where they surrendered what remained of the city to the Union on September 2, 1864.

## Racial Division Unites Black Atlanta

By the 1870s, newly emancipated African Americans constituted almost half of Atlanta's population but after federal troops withdrew from the city in 1877, they lost all political power, including the right to vote, and saw the reemergence of legislatively mandated racial segregation.

In the face of these setbacks, African Americans did what they did best—they turned inward and formed their own communities, helping one another survive and eventually thrive by effectively harnessing polarizing social forces to their advantage. The divisive social segregation in effect following reconstruction led former slaves to begin purchasing property east of the city in the area of Wheat Street (now Auburn Avenue) and Butler Street (now Jesse Hill Jr. Drive). By 1881, the year Spelman College was founded, Butler Street was central to a largely African-American community derisively known as "Darktown."

This community prospered, especially along a social and commercial artery that became known as Sweet Auburn Avenue. Prosperity and pride were the keys to racial progress in Atlanta and led to the establishment of several powerful churches, such as Ebenezer Baptist Church, which provided their members with religious, financial, and political educations. And within the sanctuary walls of activist churches such as Friendship Baptist and Big Bethel Baptist, early homes were provided to historic black colleges that were founded in Atlanta or relocated there in their infancy.

In the case of Morehouse College, which moved from the basement of Atlanta's Friendship Baptist Church in 1879, the church provided for the school; and in turn the school produced preachers as the community leaders and social activists, which graced the church's pulpit. The largesse of its well-off membership's offerings funded facilities, furnishings, and books, among other needs.

This increasingly affluent and educated black populace then began to push for equal rights and the ballot. Although the push began in the churches, the banner was carried by the students. The Atlanta University Center, founded in 1929, became home to the emerging student-led protest movement fighting for the civil rights of oppressed and disenfranchised African Americans. They were urged on by ministers and activists such as Dr. Martin Luther King, Jr., who in delivering the Founders' Day address at Spelman College in 1960 proclaimed, "The students have taken passionate longings of the ages and filtered them in their own souls and fashioned a creative protest. It is one of the glowing epics of the time and I predict that it will win. . . . "

Three unique attributes of black Atlanta, the ABCs, generated the birthplace of the civil rights "dream": A—Auburn Avenue; the three Bs—bucks, books, and the ballot; and C—the powerful black churches. The ABCs also helped ensure the survival and success of the five historic black colleges and the university in the city of Atlanta when most states where historic black colleges existed could boast of only one. The Atlanta schools attracted the best and brightest students from across the nation. They came for the education but stayed for the economic opportunity.

***"It's almost like you can see a great hand reaching down and lifting Atlanta up, because of these colleges."***
**—Maynard Jackson**

In large part, it was the graduates of Atlanta's historic black colleges who finally brought post-Reconstruction freedom and healing to Atlanta and the nation. The Atlanta student civil rights movement was born at the University Center. Advocates such as W.E.B. Du Bois and Whitney Young nursed it. Morehouse College, Spelman College, Atlanta University, and Morris Brown were all active participants in this historic civil rights movement where students such as Lonnie King, Julian Bond, and Ruby Doris Smith Robinson attended college, mentored by movement leaders such as Morehouse graduate Dr. Martin Luther King, Jr., and pastor of West Hunter Street Baptist Church Reverend Ralph Abernathy.

## A: Auburn Avenue—What's in a Name?

Auburn Avenue was the main social and commercial artery of Atlanta's African-American community, a "grand lady" in her prime—courted, respected, and loved by everyone. The two-mile stretch offered black-owned nightclubs where Cab Calloway and Duke Ellington performed. "There were big churches, fancy restaurants, clean hotels and black-owned shops, ranging from beauty salons to clothing stores to funeral parlors. . . . Verily, the sons and daughters of Ham are applying themselves to the useful arts and professions of life."—Reverend E. R. Carter, *The Black Side of Atlanta.*

Early civil rights leader and the unofficial mayor of Auburn Avenue John Wesley Dobbs dubbed the street "Sweet Auburn Avenue," perhaps inspired by the financial opportunities the street afforded to the emerging black middle- and upper-classes, even in the face of oppressive segregation laws. Or perhaps the name was inspired by the fact that on Auburn Avenue people knew each other by name. And within her graceful social and commercial folds they could meet and greet each other with the personal and political news of their insulated community. Regardless of the inspiration for the name, today "Sweet Auburn Avenue" is a name symbolic of the post-Reconstruction development of black business in Atlanta.

## B: Bucks

By the turn of the century, Auburn Avenue, the thriving economic and commercial epicenter of African-American life in Atlanta, hosted 64 black-owned businesses and the offices of several black professionals. Money earned outside the community was almost always brought to and circulated within the community. Atlanta Life Insurance, the first black-owned life insurance company founded by former slave Alonzo Franklin Herndon, and black-owned Citizens Trust Bank flourished on Sweet Auburn Avenue. Herndon's success was a brilliant reflection of all that The Avenue represented, a place where a poor country boy could lift himself up and bring others along for the ride. And oh, what a ride it was!

Born into slavery just seven years before the Civil War ended, Herndon began training as a barber at age 20 in Senoia, Georgia. He moved to Atlanta upon being offered a position by the black proprietor of Dougherty Hutchins's barbershop, which catered to a wealthy, white clientele, and he became a partner less than a year later (and the shop's name was officially changed to Hutchins & Herndon). In 1893, he married Adrienne Elizabeth McNeil, a graduate and faculty member of Atlanta University, where she taught elocution and drama.

In 1902, he opened a barber shop at 66 Peachtree Street, around the corner from Auburn Avenue. One of Atlanta's most elegant establishments, it featured crystal chandeliers, gilt-framed mirrors and fittings, massive front doors of solid mahogany, and beveled plate glass. Known from Richmond all the way to Mobile as "the best barbershop in the South," it became an unofficial city attraction visited by local Atlantans as well as tourists who reveled in its opulence. Despite his success, however, Jim Crow laws in Georgia forced Herndon to ride in the back of the streetcar that took him to work. When he arrived at the Crystal Palace, where he served a white clientele, Jim Crow legislation forced Herndon to enter his own establishment through the back door; and he was not permitted to be served on its premises during business hours. His bold response was to create a back entrance to the Crystal Palace that was the same as the front.

Herndon rose above the inherent inequities of segregation to build a real estate and business empire that included the Atlanta Life Insurance Company, one of the nation's premier African American businesses. Through it, Herndon earned money from rich white patrons who came through the front door of his palatial, racially segregated barbershop, and took those earnings out through the back door and invested it in the black community, such as his acquisition of over a hundred residential houses, along with a large commercial block of properties.

In addition to Herndon's barbershop, Sweet Auburn Avenue boasted several other precedent-setting black businesses, as enumerated by civil rights leader John Wesley Dobbs who was born just 17 years after the Civil

War. He would later recall arriving in Atlanta in 1897, "when the old artesian well still stood at Five Points," and living to see Atlanta and the state of Georgia "rise above the ruin and devastation of war to places of power and importance in this nation of ours."

During an address to the Atlanta Metropolitan Planning Commission in 1952, he recounted the contributions made by African Americans to Atlanta's rapid growth, saying, "Negroes own at least 90 percent of the property on Auburn Avenue . . . where they erected churches, brick buildings and substantial businesses. . . . It is true that we are a poor people, liberated only 85 years ago, without education or money; and yet in the last 50 years we have acquired property along Auburn Avenue, built businesses like the Atlanta Life Insurance Company, which now has more than $25,000,000 in assets; the Citizens Trust Company, a member of the Federal Reserve Banking System, with more than $5,000,000 in assets; the Atlanta Daily World, the only Negro Newspaper in America; a broadcasting station, WERD 860 on your dial, if you please."

In Atlanta, Dobbs had worked at Dr. James McDougal's Drugstore at the corner of Piedmont and Houston Streets while attending Atlanta Baptist College (Morehouse College). After passing the U.S. postal exam in 1903, he left school to become a postal clerk, a highly respected position for a turn-of-the-century black man. Three years later he married Irene Ophelia Thompson, and together they would have six daughters, all of whom graduated from Spelman College.

## B: Books and the Ballot

Despite their wealth and position, most black businessmen could not vote and chafed under the oppressive, demeaning Jim Crow laws that impacted every aspect of their daily lives. The most onerous burden was that their children were trapped in substandard public schools and were taught from outdated textbooks cast off from white schools. It was their quest for useful books for their children that pushed African Americans to fight for the ballot as a means of effecting change.

On February 12, 1936, John Wesley Dobbs gave a two-hour speech at

**The King Family: Martin is third from left.**
*(Courtesy Morehouse College Archives)*

Big Bethel Church to awaken the political conscience of 90,000 black Atlantans. Immediately following that speech he organized the Atlanta Civic and Political League to register 10,000 voters. It would become the first political action organization for black voters. He single-handedly trained black voters to successfully complete the racially biased registration process and escorted them to the polls, often paying the poll tax—created by white legislators to deter the black vote—himself. These efforts dramatically elevated the number of black voters from a few hundred to thousands. The ballot was the key to improving the living conditions of black Atlantans, and especially black public schools.

On the front lines of this expanded battle for the ballot was the dynastic King family, three generations of Morehouse men who gave Atlanta three generations of church and civil rights leaders.

## THE REVEREND ALFRED DANIEL WILLIAMS

The King family's legacy as a religious and political powerhouse began with the Reverend Alfred Daniel Williams, the maternal grandfather of Martin Luther King, Jr. The second pastor of Ebenezer Baptist Church, he was an early pioneer of "social gospel," effectively combining the strategy for social advancement of Booker T. Washington, which emphasized black business development, with that of W.E.B. Du Bois, which called for immediate equal civil rights, a message well received by Atlanta's burgeoning middle and upper middle classes.

Early in 1917, A. D. Williams joined Atlanta University graduate Walter White in an initiative to organize a local branch of the National Association for the Advancement of Colored People (NAACP).

Upon chartering the branch, a successful campaign was initiated to impede the Board of Education's plan to close seventh grade classes in black schools in order to pay for a new junior high school for white students. However, subsequent petitions to improve the conditions of existing black schools were unheeded by the school board.

In a strongly worded petition, an NAACP committee led by John Hope, the first black president of Morehouse College and his wife, Lugenia Burns, it was argued, "You, with fifty schools, most of them ample, efficient and comfortable, for the education of your children, can square neither your conscience with your God nor your conduct with your oaths, and behold Negro children in fourteen unsanitary, dilapidated, unventilated school rooms, with double sessions in half of the grades, no industrial facilities, no preparation for high school and no high schools for the blacks."

A year later Williams was elected president of the NAACP and set about recruiting new members. Within five months the branch grew by 1400 members and immediately began registering black voters to challenge a local referendum on school taxes and bond issues for public works, which would allocate a disproportionate share of raised funds to black schools. The 2,500 black Atlantans who paid the poll tax and overcame other voter registration obstacles ably defeated the education measures twice. In March 1920, women were granted the vote and black voter registration more than doubled in two years. This larger, united black voting block convinced white community leaders to make a firm commitment to the black community. A new type of power sharing was born, one which would benefit all Atlantans. A new bond issue—with several million dollars earmarked to build eighteen new schools, including four black elementary schools and Atlanta's first public high school for black students—was overwhelmingly passed with a record turnout. Williams's grandson, Dr. Martin Luther King, Jr., would receive most of his public education in two of the new schools, David T. Howard Elementary School and Booker T. Washington High School.

*The Atlanta Independent* later reported that "[it] was the ballot that gave Atlanta Negroes modern . . . schoolhouses and facilities; and it was the inspiration that the race received from the local branch under the leadership of Dr. A. D. Williams that put the fight in their bones."

## MARTIN LUTHER KING, SR.

In the year prior to successful passage of the bond issue a young, itinerant, barely literate preacher, Martin (then Michael) Luther King, Sr., moved from rural Georgia to Atlanta, where his life soon became inextricably linked with that of the city's most prominent Baptist preacher. Michael King met the only child of A. D. Williams while visiting his sister "Woodie," who boarded with the family on Auburn Avenue. When they met, sixteen-year-old Alberta Williams, a member of Atlanta's black aristocracy, was enrolled in Spelman Seminary's four-year high school program. Despite their age difference, the twenty-three-year-old King was soon attracted by Alberta's "gracious manners, captivating smile and scholarly manner." The mutual attraction resulted in a courtship, which persisted despite her father's insistence that she enroll in the Hampton Normal and Industrial Institute teaching program in Virginia.

Following graduation, Alberta returned to Atlanta. In 1924, the couple's engagement was announced at Ebenezer Baptist Church during Sunday services. On Thanksgiving Day 1926, the Reverend Michael (later known as "Martin Luther" King, Senior) and Alberta Christine Williams were married at Ebenezer in a service conducted by three of Atlanta's most prominent black Baptist ministers: Reverend Peter Bryant of Wheat Street, E. R. Carter of Friendship, and James M. Nabrit of Mt. Olive.

The couple took up residence in the Williamses' fifteen-room Victorian family home and had three children, Willie Christine, (Michael) Martin Luther, Jr., and Alfred Daniel, within their first four years of marriage. Following A. D. Williams's death, King Sr. took over his father-in-law's ministry and rescued Ebenezer Baptist from financial disaster precipitated by the Great Depression.

In 1934, King, who like his father-in-law was now a graduate of the Morehouse School of Religion and a recognized and respected pastor in his own right, traveled to the World Baptist Alliance in Berlin and changed his name and that of his son to Martin Luther King. As pastor of one of the largest and most influential churches in Atlanta, he, like his father-in-law before him, led the fight for racial equality—heading both the Atlanta Civic and Political League and the city's NAACP branch. His greatest impact, however, was probably made at the Kings' family home where King Sr. and his robust family continued to reside until shortly after his mother-in-law's death.

Whether in or out of the pulpit, the elder King's life was a civil rights sermon in which he actively resisted racial segregation and discrimination. In the community, he did not permit his children to attend segregated theatres and endure the humiliation of being treated as second-class citizens. At home, King Sr. expressed disdain for "the ridiculous nature of segregation in the South" during dinnertime discussions. And after dinner, King Sr. met with the most respected civil rights leaders of his day, raised socially conscious children and stressed the need for an educated, politically active ministry, often calling for "God to hasten the time when every minister will become a registered voter and a part of every movement for the betterment of our people."

## MARTIN LUTHER KING, JR.

King Jr., known as "M.L." or "Mike" to his friends, answered his father's call, enduring beatings and arrests to march into history as perhaps the most compelling civil rights leader ever. While "I Have a Dream" is perhaps his best remembered speech, "Give Us the Ballot"—the leitmotif of a 1957 speech at the Lincoln Memorial before 20,000 people—became the battle cry of African Americans responding to the failure of cities and states to implement the decision in *Brown v. Board of Education* "with all deliberate speed" as mandated by the U.S. Supreme Court.

On May 17, 1957, in an effort to prod the federal government into enforcing the Supreme Court's three-year-old *Brown* decision, 28-year-old Morehouse College graduate Martin Luther King, Jr., and national civil rights leaders such as Bayard Rustin, Ella Baker, A. Philip Randolph, Stanley Levison, and Adam Clayton Powell, among others, had answered the pilgrimage call.

Speaking last and perhaps remembering his father's dinner conversations, King urged the president and every member of Congress to give African Americans the right to vote so that we would not have to bother "the federal government about our basic rights." Pressing on he implored them to "give us the ballot and we will fill the legislative halls of Congress with men who will not sign a 'Southern Manifesto' because of their devotion to the manifesto of justice. Give us the ballot and we will put judges on the benches of the South who will do justice and love mercy."

> ***"Throughout the afternoon of May 17, 1957, the air was filled with shouts of 'amen' and 'hallelujah' as the speakers sounded their voices in defense of civil rights. Handkerchiefs flew above the heads of the crowd as it listened to the fiery orators. . . . There were jubilant sounds . . . sounds of disillusioned souls discovering their country."***
>
> **—Harold Sims, correspondent for the U.S. National Student Association**

Eventually the ballot was won, but only at great personal sacrifice. In true Pauline tradition, patriots such as Dr. Martin Luther King, Jr., were "hard pressed on every side, but not crushed; perplexed, but not in despair; persecuted but not abandoned. Struck down, but not destroyed." (The Apostle Paul, 2 Corinthians 4:8–10) When beaten down with batons of injustice, they got up again.

The determination and resilience of these foot soldiers was most clearly demonstrated in Selma, Alabama, on March 7, 1965, "Bloody Sunday." Civil rights activists attempting to march to the state capitol in Montgomery were beaten back by troopers with billy clubs and tear gas before they could cross Selma's Edmund Pettus Bridge.

The police brutality against these peaceful protestors took place in full view of the national media, turning the tide of public opinion in favor of the activists, and President Lyndon Johnson signed the Voting Rights Act of 1965 in August of that year. The act suspended (and amendments to the act later banned) the use of literacy tests and other qualification tests to prevent blacks from registering to vote. The ballot ardently sought and fought for by three generations of the King dynasty, among others, was finally won!

## C: Churches

According to King Jr., "the church has always been a second home for me." Likewise, for thousands of black Atlantans, the local black churches provided a second home in the years immediately following emancipation and beyond.

Following the Civil War the American Missionary Association (AMA) sent waves of teachers to the war-ravaged South to Christianize and educate former slaves, ill-equipped to face the future. By 1900, Atlanta boasted nearly a dozen black Baptist churches. In serving the spiritual and secular needs of the evolving black community, many of these churches became directly involved in the struggle for racial justice. When blacks were denied burial in Atlanta's Oakland Cemetery, several church leaders organized the South View Cemetery for blacks. In 1904 Reverend Peter J. Bryant of Wheat Street Baptist Church organized the Atlanta Benevolent and Protective Association, a small insurance society for blacks who were sick or in need of "a decent burial." This modest beginning was the forerunner to Alonzo Herndon's highly successful Atlanta Life Insurance Company.

As black churches became increasingly concerned with the secular needs of their growing congregations their relationship with black educational institutions continued to expand.

### FRIENDSHIP BAPTIST CHURCH

Friendship Baptist Church, Atlanta's first black Baptist independent congregation, has enjoyed a unique role in educating black Atlanta, extending its hand and facilities to three of the six educational institutions comprising the Atlanta University Center. Unable to purchase property, the congregation began worshipping in a boxcar, sharing these facilities with a school for former slaves that later became Atlanta University. At the invitation of the Rev. Frank Quarles, both the Augusta Institute—originally founded in the basement of Augusta's Springfield Baptist Church—and Spelman College found a home in the basement of the Atlanta church. Augusta Institute changed its name to Atlanta Baptist Seminary and today is Morehouse College, located on a 66-acre campus near historic West End in Atlanta. Both Morehouse and Spelman enjoy an international reputation for producing leaders who have influenced national and world history, among them prominent civil rights leaders.

### BIG BETHEL A.M.E. CHURCH

Like Morehouse, Spelman, and Atlanta University, Morris Brown College in Atlanta also had its beginnings in a black church, Big Bethel A.M.E. Church. Founded in 1847, the church later played a major role in the civil rights movement and boasts the oldest African-American congregation in the metropolitan Atlanta area.

### WHEAT STREET BAPTIST CHURCH

Wheat Street Baptist Church, founded in 1869, was named for the street where it stands (later named Auburn Avenue). Once known as one of the largest black congregations in the South, Wheat Street was a pioneer in the black church movement for economic development. In the early days of the civil rights movement, strategists met at Wheat Street Baptist.

### BUTLER STREET C.M.E. CHURCH

Butler Street C.M.E. Church dates from 1882 and is Atlanta's oldest Christian Methodist Episcopal church. Organized by the late Reverend S. E. Poe in 1882, it grew out of a Sunday school that operated on Gilmer Street. Today, the Butler Street C.M.E. Church is listed on the register of national historic sites.

# Acknowledgments

WITH DEEPEST RESPECT and appreciation to Richard Ember, one of the finest editors in the business. Your professional skill in revising this edition of *Southern Homecoming Traditions* has brought the rich food heritage of Atlanta to the forefront, while providing the equally amazing history as a wonderfully seasoned backdrop. Thank you also for championing this book, which "edutains" readers who may open it for a recipe and find themselves savoring the delicious tidbits of history.

I appreciate you and the professional staff of Kensington more than you may ever know. Although I am privileged to have my name on the cover, I know that there were numerous behind-the-scene hours spent bringing this book into production. I especially appreciate the support of Jessica McClelland, now retired, and miss her tremendously.

Please accept my heartfelt Thank you!

# Introduction

*Southern Homecoming Traditions* is a cookbook incorporating the history of the five historic black colleges and one university that constitute the Atlanta University Center (AUC). In the South a homecoming is a celebration of family. Most often it is a celebration of kinship involving only our families of birth. However, it can also reunite our families of choice—church, friends, and college classmates with whom we share a kindred spirit. When we come home we jubilantly celebrate our common root of kinship with wonderful food that reminds us of what we missed while away, each one bringing a special dish to the table. We also share the stories that unite and inspire us. In this way we honor those who have gone before us and guide the generations that follow as together we celebrate our "roots and wings." The collection of recipes found here is not uniquely southern but also celebrates the culinary diversity of the "new Atlanta." Each new family member has brought a unique dish to the table, as evidenced by the ubiquitous ethnic restaurants that are infusing so-called traditional southern food with a distinct and irresistible flavor. *Southern Homecoming Traditions* further celebrates the manner in which the AUC embraced these differences and its active role in unifying a once divided city, state, and nation. This unique partnership played a significant and historic role in the rebuilding of Atlanta as an economic and social leader of the new South.

The AUC began in 1929 when three schools—Atlanta University (chartered 1867), Morehouse College, a liberal arts college for men (1867), and Spelman College, a liberal arts school for women (1881)—agreed to become affiliated in a university plan. In accordance with this agreement, Atlanta University became exclusively dedicated to graduate education, while Morehouse and Spelman continued to provide undergraduate programs for AUC students. Later Clark College (chartered 1877); Morris Brown College, a coeducational college (1885); Interdenominational Theological Center, a federation of six seminaries (1958); and Morehouse School of Medicine (1983), the newest member, became affiliated with the Atlanta University Center. In 1988 Clark College and Atlanta University merged to form Clark Atlanta University and retained its affiliation with the AUC. Together, this consortium of six independent institutions constitutes the largest historically black educational complex in the world and is a tribute to the sense of unity of its founding members.

The AUC constituents enjoy an impeccable academic reputation. When *Black Enterprise Magazine* announced its pick of the "50 best colleges and universities for African Americans in 2003," three AUC institutions were in the top ten. Morehouse was ranked number 1; its sister school Spelman was ranked number 3, and Clark Atlanta came in at number 10. The AUC is rivaled only by Washington D.C.'s Howard University as the producer of the most black postgraduates.

Taught by civil rights leaders such as W.E.B. Du Bois, Whitney Young, and Dr. Benjamin E. Mays, Morehouse and Spelman alumni include movement leaders such as Dr. Martin Luther King, Jr., Lonnie King, Julian Bond, Ruby Doris Smith Robinson, and Marian Wright Edelman, among others. Morehouse men and Spelman women, joined by other AUC students, were in the forefront of a national movement that forever changed the face of a nation, while repeatedly resurrecting Atlanta from the ashes of a divisive and destructive conflict and returning her to a preeminent position as a major commercial and cultural center. In doing so, they created a "New South," one in which power sharing among blacks and whites produced economic opportunities for everyone. This economic growth and power sharing is in large part due to the AUC producing more African-American graduates than any other city in the world. And for the most part this educated populace has remained in Atlanta, creating opportunities for themselves and their communities while helping to rebuild a city once hopelessly divided over the issues of slavery and equal rights.

*Southern Homecoming Traditions* celebrates the success of this unique partnership and tells the story of courageous AUC students, already united in an academic consortium, now united in a civil rights movement to ensure equal rights for all Atlantans and Americans. The capstone of that united effort is found in their ability to remain united while sharing power to create a better Atlanta.

In the tradition of *The African-American Heritage Cookbook, A Taste of Freedom,* and *Celebrating Our Equality, Southern Homecoming Traditions* is more than a cookbook. It is a unique collection of recipes, vintage photographs, and historic narrative that shares the story of a once oppressed people's academic and economic triumph as they forged the iron bars of segregation into a strong black economic foundation and then expanded it to provide increased economic opportunities for all Atlantans. The schools on the cutting edge of Atlanta's socioeconomic transformation remain as relevant today as the day they were founded. Committed to their mission, they are strongly rooted in a historically rich and relevant heritage. Their growth is synonymous with that of the new Atlanta, whose skyline is one of the most recognizable in the country. Their union, formed to overcome the divisions caused by slavery, war, and segregation, has bound them together as a family of choice. This unity and commitment to a better Atlanta for all Atlantans has brought the city full circle, reuniting its population in such a way as to give cause for a Southern homecoming celebration!

# Morehouse College

*To engage in conflict, one does not bring a knife that cuts—but a needle that sews.*
—African proverb

*"1867, set like a jewel between the years of the Civil Rights Act and the Fourteenth Amendment to the United States Constitution . . . saw the beginning of Augusta Institute, later Atlanta Baptist College, now Morehouse College."*

**—"Educational Cross Roads in the South," a radio address delivered by Reverend Maynard H. Jackson, Morehouse, 1914.**

## Morehouse: The Early Years

Like a child's toys, carelessly broken and discarded, the vestiges of war were haphazardly strewn over a Southern landscape. Great guns that once boomed in defiance now stood mournfully silent, standing watch over an uneasy peace. Nearly four years had passed since the ground was consecrated at Gettysburg and only three since the Great Emancipator was laid to a hero's rest.

The year 1867 saw the struggle of rebuilding the South's cities and economy without slave labor. In many ways the country was still bitterly engaged in a new political war over the civil rights and equal protection of former slaves.

The Thirteenth Amendment abolishing slavery had been ratified at the end of 1865. Much of the impetus for Reconstruction involved the enforcement of civil rights for freed slaves in the Southern states. The Fourteenth Amendment offered former slaves citizenship and equal protection under the law and was drafted to guarantee their rights and safety against retaliatory acts of disgruntled Southerners. Congress passed the Fourteenth Amendment in 1866 but President Johnson advised Southern states to reject it, and except for Tennessee, they did.

It was against this social and political backdrop in 1867 that Augusta Institute, the beginning of present-day Morehouse College, was founded in Augusta, Georgia, by the Reverend William Jefferson White, a Baptist minister and cabinetmaker. Supporting him in this endeavor were the Reverend

Richard C. Coulter, a former slave from Augusta, and the Reverend Edmund Turney, organizer of the National Theological Institute for Educating Freedmen in Washington, D.C.

**Reverend William Jefferson White**
*(Private collection)*

The school was established in the basement of Springfield Baptist Church (founded in Augusta in 1787, the oldest independent African-American church in America). Four difficult years followed, with threats from the Ku Klux Klan, who viewed the school's work as "infamous" and "diabolical," loss of faculty and leadership, poor facilities, and other problems. For a time the school moved to Harmony Baptist Church, pastored by Reverend White, who also taught one of the night classes. His " . . . sympathetic wife gave many a meal to hungry students and shared her

**Springfield Baptist Church**
*(Private collection)*

meager supply of house furnishings, bed covering, and even the family clothing with those that came with scarcely more than a desire to know and the determination to satisfy that desire." —Morehouse alumnus, December 1932

**Reverend Frank Quarles**
*(Private collection)*

Twelve years after its founding, the Augusta Institute, accepting the invitation of Rev. Frank Quarles, moved to the basement of Friendship Baptist Church in Atlanta and changed its name to Atlanta Baptist Seminary. Eventually, the Seminary acquired a sister school for women that ultimately became Spelman College, and after several changes of location, laid the cornerstone for its present site in Atlanta's West End community in 1889 under the administration of its second president, Dr. Samuel T. Graves.

A new era in the history of Morehouse dawned when faculty member

**Dr. Samuel Graves, the second president of Morehouse College, for whom Graves Hall was named.**
*(Courtesy Morehouse College Archives)*

**Reverend Henry L. Morehouse**

*(Private collection)*

**Graves Hall**

*(Archives and Special Collections: Robert Woodruff Library at the Atlanta University Center)*

Dr. John Hope was appointed the fourth president in 1906, the first black man to lead Morehouse College.

The new educational era was reflected in yet another change in name. Upon the death of William White in 1913, Atlanta Baptist College was named Morehouse College in honor of Henry L. Morehouse, the corresponding secretary of the Northern Baptist Home Mission Society.

On April 1, 1929, the agreement of the affiliation uniting Morehouse College, Spelman College, and Atlanta University was signed. These institutions would share resources while remaining autonomous. Each would retain individual control of its own finances, board of trustees, president, and administrative officers. With the exception of Atlanta University, each institution would nominate three members to its board, and those nominated members would then select the remaining board members. The agreement secured the future of the participating schools and eventually included three additional educational institutions to make up what is now the Atlanta University Center. Morehouse would continue providing undergraduate education to men, while Spelman continued to provide undergraduate education to women. Only Atlanta University would offer postgraduate degrees.

***"We make our living by what we get. We make our life by what we give. Whatever you do, strive to do it so well that no man living and no man dead, and no man yet to be born can do it any better. As we face the unpredictable future, have faith that man and God will assist us all the way."***

**—Dr. Benjamin E. Mays, president, Morehouse College, 1940–67**

## BENJAMIN MAYS

In 1940, Dr. Benjamin Elijah Mays, a Phi Beta Kappa graduate of Bates College and the University of Chicago, was appointed the sixth president of Morehouse College. During his 27-year tenure he elevated Morehouse to the next level in its growth by building its international reputation for excellence in scholarship, leadership, and service. The son of former slaves, Mays led a 15-million-dollar increase in donations and oversaw the construction of

**Dr. Benjamin E. Mays, son of former slaves, dean of the Howard University School of Religion, prolific author, nationally noted educator, mentor to Dr. Martin Luther King, Jr., and sixth president of Morehouse College (1940–67).**
*(Courtesy Morehouse College Archives)*

eighteen new buildings. Morehouse was increasing in strength and attracting some of the best and brightest young minds in the country.

Mays successfully integrated his Christian love of humankind with his duty to reject the hatred of racism by demanding God's justice for all people. He encouraged Morehouse men to stand strong in accepting nothing less than full equality. During his tenure the term "Morehouse man" came to define young black men as confident, intelligent, and honest leaders. Mays once said, "There is an air of expectancy at Morehouse College. It is expected that the student who enters here will do well. It is also expected that once a man bears the insignia of a Morehouse graduate he will do exceptionally well. We expect nothing less." —Benjamin Mays, charge to the graduating class of 1961.

Among the students Mays inspired "to do exceptionally well" was Martin Luther King, Jr. In 1948, during one of Mays' Tuesday morning chapel addresses, he introduced King Jr. to Gandhi's philosophy of nonviolence—a philosophy King would courageously use in the struggle to free his race from the bondage of Jim Crow segregation. With a shared commitment to non-violent social change, a friendship soon blossomed between Mays and King. When King won the Nobel Peace Prize in 1964, it was Mays who organized a successful citywide celebration in Atlanta for his protégé and friend. When King was assassinated just four years later, Mays gave

**Morehouse men at chapel service.**
*(Courtesy Morehouse College Archives)*

the eulogy. Dr. King once remembered Dr. Mays as his "spiritual mentor" and "intellectual father," and King's legacy has resulted in Dr. Benjamin Elijah Mays being remembered as one of the most influential educators of twentieth-century America.

Today, as Morehouse celebrates 139 years of challenge and change, the college continues to deliver an exceptional educational experience that meets the intellectual, moral, and social needs of students representing more than 40 states and 18 countries—a unique institution dedicated, as always, to producing outstanding men and extraordinary leaders to serve humanity with a spiritual consciousness.

Morehouse is perhaps best known for the achievements of its distinguished alumni, including Martin Luther King, Jr., Olympian Edwin Moses, filmmaker Spike Lee, former mayor of Atlanta Maynard Jackson, activist Julian Bond, and several United States congressmen. Morehouse men were often the college's best recruiters.

# *Appetizers*

**An appetizer is offered before a meal to stimulate a desire for more. Such was the case with Morehouse College, which inspired its own future growth and that of the many Atlanta University Colleges and University that followed in its footsteps.**

## Sweet Auburn Avenue Wings

Once known as the hub of black Atlanta, in its heyday Auburn Avenue was recognized by *Forbes* magazine as the "richest Negro street in America." It is also the birthplace of Dr. Martin Luther King, Jr.

Served piping hot or at room temperature, these succulent wings will be the hit of your party. The unusual blend of aromatic flavors will have you playing Twenty Questions with your guests as they try to guess the ingredients. Start preparing this dish one day in advance to allow your wings to marinate 24 hours before baking them.

**5 pounds chicken wings**
**1½ cups freshly squeezed orange juice**
**¼ cup freshly squeezed lime juice**
**3 tablespoons freshly grated orange zest**
**1 teaspoon grated lime zest**
**1½ cups pineapple juice**
**1½ cups honey**
**¾ cup soy sauce**
**7 garlic cloves, minced**
**1 teaspoon cayenne pepper (or to taste)**
**Salt**
**Freshly ground black pepper**

Rinse the chicken wings, pat dry, and set aside. In a large bowl, combine the remaining ingredients and mix to blend. Add the chicken wings to the marinade and turn well to coat. Cover tightly and refrigerate for at least 24 hours and up to 2 days, turning occasionally to coat with the marinade. Preheat the oven to 400°F. Line two large baking sheets with aluminum foil. Arrange the wings on the baking sheets in a single layer. Bake for 15 minutes, baste with any leftover marinade, and turn basted wings over. Bake the wings for 15 to 20 minutes or until they are cooked through and golden brown. Serve hot or at room temperature.

*Makes 6 servings.*

# Peach Street Wings with Peach Mustard Sauce

Peach Street is one of Atlanta's main thoroughfares; however, you needn't travel that far to enjoy these soul-satisfying wings!

**3 pounds chicken wings**
**2 teaspoons dry mustard**
**1 1/4 teaspoons dried thyme**
**1 teaspoon brown sugar**
**1 1/4 teaspoons cayenne pepper**
**3/4 teaspoon salt**
**1/4 teaspoon black pepper**
**1/4 cup lemon juice**

Cut tips off wings; reserve for stock. Wash under cold running water and set aside to drain. In small bowl, combine the remaining ingredients to make a paste. Use a pastry brush to brush the paste over the wings. Arrange the wings, meaty side down, on lightly greased foil-lined baking sheets and allow to stand for 30 minutes at room temperature. Preheat the oven to 475°F. Place wings in oven and bake for 15 minutes; turn wings over and bake for an additional 15 to 20 minutes or until brown, crisp, and no longer pink inside.

*Makes 12 servings.*

### PEACH MUSTARD SAUCE

The secret's in the sauce.

**1/2 cup peach jam**
**1 tablespoon Dijon-style mustard**
**1 teaspoon cider vinegar**
**4 cloves garlic, minced**
**2 teaspoons paprika**

Place jam in a saucepan; cook and stir over low heat. Add remaining ingredients and stir until melted and well-blended, approximately 3 to 4 minutes. Serve separately as a dipping sauce for the wings.

*Makes about 1/2 cup of sauce.*

## Honey & Spice Wings

Mmmmm. These spicy morsels will keep your guests guessing about the identities of the exotic ingredients that suffuse these tantalizing wings with unique flavor.

**3 pounds chicken drummettes**
**Salt and pepper**
**1 cup honey**
**2 tablespoons curry powder**
**1 teaspoon ground ginger**
**1/8 teaspoon ground cumin**
**1/2 teaspoon cayenne pepper, or to taste**

Preheat oven to 400°F. Rinse drummettes under cold running water, pat dry, salt and pepper to taste, and arrange in single layer on a baking sheet. Place drummettes in the preheated oven and bake for 10 minutes. While the drummettes are baking, combine the remaining ingredients in a small bowl and mix until well blended. Remove drummettes from the oven and brush them with half of the honey mixture; bake an additional 10 minutes. Use tongs to turn the drummettes over, brush them with the remaining honey mixture, and bake an additional 10 minutes. Cool slightly at room temperature before serving.

*Makes 6 to 8 servings.*

# Jamaican Jerk Hot Wings

"Yah-mahn." Jerk, a method of cooking attributed to the Carib-Arawak Indians, imparts a sweet and spicy smoke flavor to meat. After thoroughly cleaning captured game, the Indians "jerked" the animal's flesh with sharp objects and filled the openings created by jerking the meat with a variety of aromatic spices. It was then placed in a deep, stone-lined pit and covered with green wood which, when burned, smoked heavily, adding to the rich flavor of the superb results: a spicy, moist, and tender meat dish.

**5 pounds fresh chicken wings or drumettes (do not use frozen)**
**1 tablespoon ground allspice**
**1 1/4 teaspoons salt**
**1 1/2 tablespoons dried thyme**
**1 3/4 teaspoons cayenne pepper**
**1 teaspoon freshly ground black pepper**
**1 1/2 teaspoons ground sage**
**3/4 teaspoon ground nutmeg**
**3/4 teaspoon ground cinnamon**
**2 tablespoons finely grated fresh garlic**
**1 tablespoon brown sugar**
**1/4 cup olive oil**
**1/4 cup soy sauce**
**1/2 cup white vinegar**
**1/4 cup pineapple juice**
**1/2 cup orange juice**
**1/2 cup lime juice**

**2 tablespoons grated ginger**
**2 habañero (or Scotch bonnet) peppers, seeded and chopped**
**4 green onions, finely chopped**

Wash drummettes under cold running water and set aside to drain. In a large bowl, combine the allspice, thyme, cayenne pepper, black pepper, sage, nutmeg, cinnamon, salt, garlic, and brown sugar. With a wire whisk, slowly add the olive oil, soy sauce, vinegar, pineapple juice, orange juice, lime juice, and grated ginger. Add the Scotch bonnet pepper and onions, and mix well. Add the chicken wings, cover, and marinate for at least 3 to 4 hours, or longer if possible.

Preheat an outdoor grill.

Remove the wings from the marinade and grill for 3 to 4 minutes on each side or until fully cooked. While grilling, baste with the marinade. Bring the leftover marinade to a rapid boil. Boil 5 to 6 minutes, remove from heat, and serve on the side for dipping.

*Note:* The Scotch bonnet pepper or habañero is the hottest of the capsicum peppers. It is truly incendiary, and therefore should be approached with extreme caution. Wear gloves when handling it and wash hands thoroughly after use. Whatever you do, do not put unwashed hands anywhere near your face. If habañeros are unavailable, or if my warnings have left you quaking in your culinary boots, substitute serrano, Thai bird chiles, or jalapeño peppers. Serve the finished dish immediately with lots of very cold beer.

*Makes 10 to 12 servings.*

# Jamaican Shrimp

**2½ pounds large fresh shrimp in shells**
**¼ cup salad oil**
**3 tablespoons white wine vinegar**
**3 tablespoons lime juice**

**2 jalapeño peppers, seeded and finely chopped**
**1 tablespoon honey**
**2 1/2 teaspoons Quick Jamaican Jerk Seasoning (see recipe below)**
**1 medium mango, pitted, peeled, sliced, and halved crosswise**
**1 small lime, halved crosswise and sliced**
**1 small red onion, quartered and thinly sliced**

Place shrimp in lightly salted boiling water for 1 to 3 minutes or until shrimp turn pink and the tails begin to turn. Drain immediately and cool under cold running water. Peel shrimp, leaving tails intact, and devein. Place shrimp in a heavy plastic bag. At this point, you can seal the bag and chill for up to 24 hours.

Next, prepare the marinade by combining the salad oil, white wine vinegar, lime juice, jalapeño pepper, honey, and the Jamaican Jerk Seasoning in a screw-top-covered jar. Cover and shake well to mix. Pour over shrimp in plastic bag, reseal the bag, and chill for 1 1/2 to 2 hours, turning bag occasionally.

To serve, pour shrimp and marinade into a large serving bowl and garnish the sides with alternating slices of sliced mango, limes, and onions.

*Makes 10 to 12 appetizer servings.*

## QUICK JAMAICAN JERK SEASONING

**2 teaspoons onion powder**
**1 teaspoon sugar**
**1 teaspoon ground thyme**
**1 teaspoon salt**
**1/2 teaspoon ground allspice**
**1/4 teaspoon ground cinnamon**
**1/4 teaspoon ground nutmeg**
**1/4 teaspoon cayenne pepper**
**1/4 teaspoon ground cumin**

Combine the above ingredients and mix well.

# Rum-Glazed Tiger Prawns

A mouth-watering treat, these delectable prawns will have your guests circling the grill for more.

**3 pounds fresh tiger prawns**
**3/4 cup light rum, divided**
**1/4 cup + 2 tablespoons fresh lime juice**
**1/4 cup vegetable oil**
**4 large garlic cloves, minced**
**1/2 teaspoon crushed red pepper**
**1/2 teaspoon salt**
**1/4 cup white cider vinegar**
**1/2 cup firmly packed dark brown sugar**

Peel and devein prawns, leaving tails intact. Place them in bowl with 1/4 cup of the rum, lime juice, oil, garlic, crushed red pepper, and salt; toss to coat thoroughly. Cover; refrigerate, and allow to marinate for 1 hour.

Preheat grill according to manufacturer's instructions. In small bowl, combine brown sugar, vinegar, and remaining 2 tablespoons of the rum. Thread shrimp on skewers; lightly brush with brown sugar glaze.

Grill over a medium-hot fire about 3 minutes per side, brushing with additional glaze, until shrimp are opaque.

*Note:* If using bamboo skewers, soak them in water for 30 minutes before grilling.

*Makes 6 to 8 servings.*

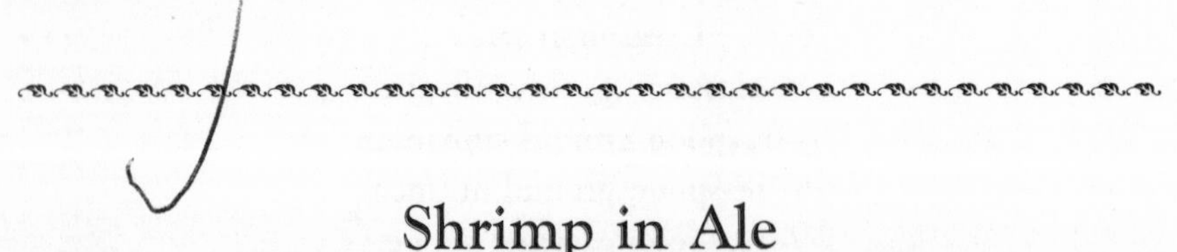

# Shrimp in Ale

**3 pounds large shrimp (20–24 count per pound)**
**36 ounces beer**
**8 large garlic cloves, peeled and crushed**
**1/4 cup Seafood Seasoning (see recipe opposite)**

**2 tablespoons salt**
**3 bay leaves**
**4 teaspoons Tabasco**
**1 1/2 teaspoons celery seed**
**2 teaspoons cayenne pepper**
**Juice of 2 lemons**
**Melted butter seasoned to taste with additional Seafood Seasoning**

Wash shrimp, but do not remove the shells. Combine the remaining ingredients except the lemon juice and butter in a saucepan and bring to a rapid boil. Add shrimp and bring to a second boil. Reduce heat to low and simmer uncovered until shrimp are pink and tender, approximately 2 to 3 minutes. Drain. Combine lemon juice and butter and serve shrimp hot with melted lemon butter. Yields 60 to 72 shrimp.

### SEAFOOD SEASONING

**2 tablespoons celery salt**
**1 tablespoon ground bay leaves**
**1 tablespoon salt**
**1 1/2 teaspoons paprika**
**1 teaspoon onion powder**
**1 teaspoon dry mustard**
**1 1/2 teaspoons garlic powder**
**1 teaspoon cayenne pepper**
**1 teaspoon ground nutmeg**
**1 teaspoon dried oregano**
**1 teaspoon ground thyme**
**3/4 teaspoon ground cloves**
**1/4 teaspoon ground allspice**

Combine the above ingredients, mix well, and store in an airtight container until ready for use.

*Makes approximately 1/2 cup.*

# Garlic Herb Mussels

This is a wonderful appetizer. Mussels may come already cleaned, but cleaning fresh mussels is not as intimidating as it appears to be. In fact, it's really simple. Place the mussels in a pot, cover them with water, and stir a cup or two of cornmeal into the water. Let sit for a couple of hours. During this time, the shellfish will eliminate any sand (the technique works equally well for clams). Every fifteen minutes or so, jostle the bowl to create a wave. This stimulates them to ingest cornmeal and expel sand. To debeard a mussel, simply grab hold of the black stringy "beard" sticking out of the shell (not all mussels will have these) and yank! That's all there is to it.

This very traditional and simple recipe is a wonderful way to prepare mussels. The best part is that the mussels can be prepared well in advance and quickly reheated just before serving, making them perfect for parties and busy holiday dinners.

**2 pounds mussels in the shell**
**1/2 cup butter, softened**
**4 garlic cloves, minced**
**1/4 cup chopped fresh parsley**
**1/4 cup chopped fresh chives**
**2 tablespoons chopped fresh dill**

If not already cleaned, scrub and clean mussels. When using cornmeal soak to clean mussels, carefully remove the mussels from the soaking water to cook pot in batches without disturbing sand on the bottom of the bowl. Boil the mussels in batches in a large saucepan until the shells open, approximately 3 to 5 minutes. Remove each batch and boil the next until they are all cooked. Lift off the top shell of each mussel. Discard any mussel that does not open. Place the mussels in an ovenproof dish. Mix the butter, garlic, and herbs together. Spread the butter mixture evenly over the mussels and refrigerate until ready to serve. Right before serving, broil until the tops are lightly browned and aromatic.

*Makes 6 servings.*

# Hopping John Dip

**8 slices bacon**
**1 cup chopped onion**
**1/4 cup chopped green pepper**
**1 teaspoon fresh jalapeño pepper, chopped**
**1 clove garlic, peeled and minced**
**1 10-ounce package frozen black-eyed peas**
**2 cups chicken broth**
**1/2 teaspoon salt**
**1/4 cup uncooked rice**
**1 teaspoon fresh lemon juice**
**1/2 cup ham, finely chopped**
**Cayenne pepper to taste**

Fry bacon until crisp and remove to a paper towel–lined plate to drain. Reserve the bacon drippings in the frying pan, and sauté onions, green pepper, jalapeño, and garlic, stirring constantly. Cook until the onion is transparent. Add black-eyed peas, chicken broth, and salt. Cover and cook over medium heat for 15 minutes, stir in the rice, and re-cover. Reduce heat to low and cook for 25 to 30 minutes or until the rice is cooked through. Allow mixture to cool before placing it in a food processor or blender to puree. Add lemon juice. If mixture is too thick, add additional chicken broth. Garnish with bacon, chopped ham, and cayenne pepper.

*Makes 12 servings.*

## A Morehouse Moment

**Morehouse College, the nation's largest liberal arts college for men, graduates approximately 500 students each year. As a result, it confers bachelor's degrees on more black men than any other college or university in the United States.**

# Corn & Field Pea Dip

**2 15.8-ounce cans field peas with snaps, rinsed and drained**
**2 11-ounce cans white shoepeg corn, drained**
**1 1/4 cups peeled and seeded diced tomatoes**
**2 jalapeño peppers, seeded and finely minced**
**1/3 cup finely chopped onion**
**3 garlic cloves, minced**
**2 tablespoons finely chopped fresh parsley**
**1/2 cup vegetable oil**
**1/2 cup red wine vinegar**
**1/4 cup fresh lemon juice**
**1/2 teaspoon salt**

Combine the first 7 ingredients; cover and chill at least 8 hours. Whisk oil together with remaining ingredients. Drizzle over bean mixture, and toss. Chill at least 8 hours and drain immediately before serving with corn chips.

*Makes 8 cups.*

# Pickled Black-Eyed Pea Dip

**2 16-ounce cans black-eyed peas, rinsed and drained**
**2/3 cup vegetable oil**
**1/3 cup white wine vinegar**
**1 small onion, diced**
**1/2 red pepper, seeded and diced**
**1 jalapeño pepper, seeded and minced fine**
**2 garlic cloves, minced**
**1/2 teaspoon salt**
**1/8 teaspoon cayenne pepper**

Combine the above ingredients; cover and chill the mixture for at least 2 hours before serving with tortilla chips.

*Makes 5 cups.*

# Smoked Bacon & Black Bean Dip

As a general rule allow 1/4 to 1/3 cup dip per person.

**5 slices smoked bacon, fried crisp and coarsely chopped (reserve drippings)**
**1 medium onion, chopped**
**1 small red bell pepper, chopped**
**1 jalapeño pepper, stemmed, seeded, and chopped**
**1 clove garlic, minced**
**1/2 teaspoon ground cumin**
**1/2 teaspoon oregano**
**1 16-ounce can black beans, rinsed and drained**
**Salt**
**Pepper**
**1/2 cup sour cream**

Pour off all but 1 1/2 tablespoons of the bacon drippings. Add onion, red pepper, jalapeño pepper, and garlic; sauté until the onion is soft, approximately 5 to 6 minutes. Add cumin and oregano and sauté for an additional minute. Add beans with their liquid and simmer over medium-low heat until slightly thickened, about 5 minutes. Stir occasionally to prevent burning.

Remove bean mixture from heat and allow to cool for 10 minutes. Transfer 1 cup of the mixture to a blender or food processor and process until smooth. Return blended beans to bean mixture, and stir to blend. Season the dip to taste with salt and pepper. Transfer to a serving bowl and refrigerate at least 2 hours before serving. Immediately before serving, gently stir in 1/2 the bacon. Top with the sour cream and garnish with remaining bacon.

*Makes 3 cups.*

# Bacon, Tomato & Cheese Dip

**1 cup sour cream**
**2 4-ounce packages blue cheese, crumbled**
**2 3-ounce packages cream cheese, softened**
**1/4 teaspoon hot sauce**
**1/4 cup + 1 tablespoon white onion, diced**
**9 slices cooked bacon, crumbled**
**1/3 cup seeded and peeled chopped tomato**

Process the first 5 ingredients in a blender or food processor until the mixture is smooth. Stop occasionally to scrape down the sides. Stir in half of bacon and chopped tomatoes. Cover and chill 2 hours. Sprinkle with remaining bacon. Delicious served with vegetable crudités or crackers.

*Makes 1 1/2 cups.*

# Three-Onion Dip

**3 tablespoons butter**
**1 1/2 cups chopped Vidalia onion**
**2 tablespoons finely chopped red onion**
**2 tablespoons thinly sliced green onion**
**1 8-ounce carton dairy sour cream**
**1/4 teaspoon salt**
**1/4 teaspoon coarsely ground black pepper**
**1/8 teaspoon cayenne pepper**
**Heavy cream, chilled (optional)**
**1 tablespoon fresh chives, snipped**
**Assorted chips and vegetables for dipping, such as sliced fennel, baby carrots, sliced cucumbers, and sliced zucchini**

In a medium skillet melt butter over medium-high heat, and cook the onions in the butter for approximately 5 minutes or until tender. Allow onions to cool before combining them in a blender or food processor with sour cream, salt, black pepper, and cayenne pepper. Cover and blend or process until smooth. Spoon mixture into a smaller bowl; cover and chill for 1 to 24 hours. Immediately before serving, stir in cream 1 teaspoon at a time, if necessary, to adjust dipping consistency. Garnish with chives and serve with a variety of dippers, such as chips and sliced raw vegetables.

*Makes 1 1/2 cups.*

## Vidalia Onion Dip

**1 large Vidalia onion, finely chopped**
**1 cup real mayonnaise**
**1/4 teaspoon fresh lemon juice**
**1 1/4 cups grated Parmesan cheese**
**Paprika**

Preheat oven to 350°F. Lightly oil a 3-cup, oven-proof serving dish and set aside. Combine the onion, mayonnaise, lemon juice, and Parmesan cheese; mix well. Evenly spread the mixture into the prepared dish and garnish with a sprinkle of paprika. Bake in the preheated oven for 25 minutes, cool, and serve with baked pita chips.

*Makes approximately 2 1/2 cups.*

## Blooming Vidalia Onion & Dipping Sauce

**1 egg**
**1 cup milk**
**1 very large Vidalia onion**
**1 cup flour**
**1 1/2 teaspoons salt**
**1/2 teaspoon black pepper**
**1 teaspoon cayenne pepper**

**1/2 teaspoon paprika**
**1/4 teaspoon oregano**
**1/8 teaspoon ground nutmeg**
**1/8 teaspoon thyme**
**1/8 teaspoon cumin**
**Oil for deep frying**

In a medium-size bowl, combine the egg and milk, and beat well to blend. In a separate bowl, combine the next 9 dry ingredients. Slice off 1/2 to 3/4 of the top and bottom of the onion and remove skin. Cut out a 1-inch core and make slices about 3/4 of an inch down all the way around the onion to form the petals. Submerge the onion in boiling water for a minute or two to separate the petals. Remove the onion from the boiling water and set aside to cool. Next, dip the onion in the milk mixture to coat and then dip the onion in the flour mixture to coat. Repeat the dipping process and refrigerate the onion for approximately fifteen minutes to allow the coating to set. While the onion is setting, prepare the Dipping Sauce (see recipe below). Heat oil in a deep fryer according to manufacturer's directions and fry onion right side up for 10 minutes. When the onion is tender and golden brown, remove it from the deep fryer and drain on a paper towel. Serve with dipping sauce. (See recipe below.)

*Makes 2 to 4 servings, depending on the size of the onion and your guests' appetites.*

## DIPPING SAUCE

**1/2 cup mayonnaise**
**1 tablespoon ketchup**
**2 tablespoons cream-style horseradish**
**1/8 teaspoon cayenne pepper**
**1/4 teaspoon paprika**
**1/4 teaspoon salt**
**1/8 teaspoon dried oregano**

Combine the above ingredients, mix well, and refrigerate until ready to serve.

*Makes approximately 3/4 cup.*

## Martin Luther King, Jr., Morehouse '48

In September 1944, 15-year-old Martin Luther King, Jr., a future Nobel Peace Prize laureate and civil rights leader, began studies at Morehouse College in Atlanta, following in the footsteps of his father, Martin Luther King, Sr., and his grandfather, A. D. Williams. While at Morehouse he met Walter McCall, a dirt-poor student who supported himself by cutting hair for a dime in the basement of Graves Hall. King, a son of privilege, was handsomely sartorial in his dress. The two became inseparable friends. Both were quick wits and enjoyed the polysyllabic word games of Professor Gladstone Chandler, who smoked a pipe and appeared quite urbane in his tweed jackets. He encouraged flamboyant rejoinders to simple questions as a means of improving vocabulary. For instance, if Professor Chandler asked "How are you?" King, using his vast vocabulary, would fire off, "I surmise that my physical equilibrium is organically quiescent."

Word games were just one aspect of the sophomoric humor and fun shared by the "Mac and Mike" clique. (Despite the earlier name change to Martin following King Sr.'s visit to Germany, most of King's friends continued referring to him as "Mike.") Neither McCall nor King felt a specific calling to the ministry at the time, so they freely engaged in activities frowned upon by the Baptist Church such as dancing and card playing.

Martin Luther King, Jr., graduation photo. *(Courtesy Morehouse College Archives)*

# Georgia Peach Salsa & Jicama Wedges

Georgia peaches should have a creamy gold to yellow under-color. The red "blush" of a peach indicates ripeness. And as a member of the rose family it should have a sweet fragrance. Finally, it should be soft to the touch but not mushy. However, don't squeeze it because it bruises very easily!

**2 1/4 cups peeled, pitted, and coarsely chopped peaches**
**1/3 cup peeled, seeded, and chopped cucumber**
**1/3 cup chopped Bermuda onion**
**1 jalapeño pepper, stemmed, seeded, and chopped**
**2 tablespoons honey**
**3 tablespoons lime juice**
**2 tablespoons finely chopped cilantro**
**1 large tomato, seeded and finely chopped**
**Jicama wedges, 1/4-inch thick**
**Fresh lime juice**
**Fresh lime wedges**

Combine the first 8 ingredients and refrigerate to chill. Peel and slice jicama; place in a shallow dish; squeeze lime juice over the slices to prevent discoloration, and refrigerate. Serve with chilled wedges of jicama and fresh limes. Jicama, a white fleshed root vegetable, is readily available in the fresh vegetable section of your local grocery store. A good source of vitamin C, when eaten raw, it has the cool, crisp and refreshing texture of an apple. When paired with flavorful Georgia Peach Salsa, it provides a healthful alternative to chips. When shopping look for a jicama with a hard and unblemished skin. The salsa is a great accompaniment to pork and poultry dishes.

# Watermelon Salsa

Watermelon should be stored in a cool place and chilled just before serving. Once cut, it should be served within two days. Uncut, it can last as long as two weeks.

**3 tablespoons thinly sliced fresh basil**
**1/4 cup fresh lime juice**
**1 teaspoon salt**
**1/4 cup pepper**
**1 4-pound seedless watermelon, diced (approximately 6 cups)**
**3/4 cup finely chopped Bermuda onion**
**1 jalapeño pepper, seeded and finely minced (or more to taste)**
**Tortilla chips**

Combine the first four ingredients, whisk to mix well, and set aside. Drain watermelon and place it in a serving bowl with onion and jalapeño peppers, gently mix to blend. Drizzle with lime juice dressing and refrigerate 1 to 2 hours before serving with corn chips.

*Makes 6 to 8 servings.*

# Rosemary Eggplant Dip

This roasted eggplant dip will convert those most opposed to this vegetable. Its superb smoky flavor is delightful when paired with sliced vegetables, pita crisps, crackers, baguette slices, or breadsticks. The dip can be made up to two days in advance and stored tightly wrapped in the refrigerator.

**1 large eggplant**
**4 cloves garlic**
**1/2 cup sour cream**
**1/4 cup softened cream cheese**
**Salt**

**Freshly ground black pepper**
**1/8 teaspoon cumin**
**1 tablespoon chopped fresh rosemary**

Puncture eggplant with a fork several times to allow steam to escape while baking. Bake the eggplant in a 425°F oven until the skin is charred and the flesh is tender, turning occasionally. The cooking time varies depending upon the size and ripeness of the eggplant. Upon completion of cooking time, remove the eggplant from the oven and allow it to cool until it can be safely handled. Next, cut it in half and scoop out the flesh. Place the flesh in a food processor with the remaining ingredients and process until smooth. Refrigerate at least 2 hours prior to serving.

*Makes 4 servings.*

**Morehouse men dining at the home of President Benjamin Mays *(far right, seated)* and his wife, Mrs. Sadie Mays *(far left, standing).***
*(Courtesy Morehouse College Archives)*

# Hummus Bi Tahini

**2 15-ounce cans chickpeas**
**3 garlic cloves, peeled and mashed**
**1 teaspoon salt**
**1/2 teaspoon ground cumin**
**1/8 teaspoon sesame oil**
**1/3 cup olive oil**
**3 tablespoons sesame tahini (available in health food stores)**
**Juice of 3 to 4 lemons**
**Chopped parsley and cayenne pepper for garnish**
**Olive oil**
**Pita bread**

Drain chickpeas and rinse. Place well-drained chickpeas in a mixing bowl. Add mashed garlic and salt to chickpeas and mix to blend. Puree mixture in a blender or processor. Add cumin, oils, and tahini; blend. Gradually add lemon juice to taste. Mix to a fine, smooth paste. If the hummus is too thick, thin by adding a little cold water. Serve in a shallow serving dish and garnish with chopped parsley and red pepper. Offer olive oil in a separate dish and pita bread for dipping.

*Makes 12 to 18 servings.*

# Olive Spread

This quick, flavorful Mediterranean olive spread is excellent served with pieces of good crusty bread.

**3 cups whole, pitted kalamata olives**
**3 cloves garlic**
**1/3 cup olive oil**

Coarsely blend or process olives and garlic, then add olive oil in a stream while puréeing; process until mixture becomes a thick, but not too smooth, paste.

*Makes 14 servings.*

# Kalamata Caviar

A distinctive blend of magnificent flavors separates this spread from the rest. This olive, cheese, and nut mixture is delicious spread on slices of warm Cuban or French bread.

**8 ounces whole, pitted kalamata olives**
**1 4-ounce package feta cheese**
**1/2 cup chopped pistachio nuts**
**4 cloves garlic, peeled**
**Up to 2 tablespoons olive oil**

Blend or process kalamata olives, feta cheese, pistachios, garlic, and olives. Add olive oil as needed to attain a pesto-like consistency. Serve with warm Cuban or French bread.

*Makes 8 servings.*

## Maynard Holbrook Jackson, Morehouse '56

*"Morehouse was written all over Maynard Jackson. The impressive, darn near regal bearing. The courage, conviction, and morality. Jackson graduated from Morehouse in 1956, but the college never left him. It showed in the way he represented its best ideals."*

—Walter Filiker, director of the
Morehouse College Leadership Center

**Maynard H. Jackson, Jr., grandson of John Wesley Dobbs, the unofficial mayor of Auburn Avenue, and the proud great-grandson of slaves on both sides of his family tree, was swept into power by the new black majority in 1973, and would eventually serve three terms as mayor of Atlanta. He oversaw construction of what would become the nation's busiest international airport, battled a rising homeless rate, and helped attract the 1996 Olympic Games to**

A youthful Maynard Jackson.
*(Courtesy Morehouse College Archives)*

Atlanta. In addition, he established affirmative-action programs for hiring city workers and contractors and provided black neighborhoods a voice in city planning.

As mayor his crowning achievement was, as he often boasted, bringing in the Atlanta Airport "ahead of time and under budget" with significant minority contractor participation. During his administration city contracts granted to minorities soared from less than 1 percent in 1973 to nearly 39 percent within five years. As a result, Atlanta gained dozens of new black millionaires as well as a new sense of economic power-sharing from the new joint ventures arising between minority-owned companies and white-owned companies, who suddenly saw the light and the writing on the wall.

According to Michael L. Lomax, also a graduate of Morehouse College and speechwriter for Mr. Jackson in the 1970s, "When Maynard got elected . . . that's what gave black people a piece of the pie

A quintessential Morehouse man, Maynard Jackson served on the Morehouse board of trustees for 18 years. His alma mater bestowed an honorary Doctor of Laws degree upon him in 1974.
*(Courtesy Morehouse College Archives)*

**and put that city on the map for every young black person in America who had ambitions of doing something spectacular with his or her life.... In many ways," according to Lomax, "Maynard's the architect of modern Atlanta."**

# Spicy Toasted Pecans

Try this great alternative to "party peanuts" at your next cocktail social!

**1 cup pecans**
**1/4 teaspoon kosher salt**
**1/2 teaspoon paprika**
**1/4 teaspoon onion powder**
**1/8 teaspoon cayenne pepper**
**1/2 teaspoon toasted and ground cumin**
**1/2 teaspoon extra virgin olive oil**

Preheat oven to 350°F and toast pecans for 10 minutes. While pecans are toasting—watching them carefully to prevent burning—mix together the seasoning ingredients. Remove slightly browned and crispy pecans from the oven and allow them to cool slightly before tossing them in the seasoning mix. Delicious served with drinks or served alone as a snack.

*Makes 1 cup.*

# Blue Cheese & Toasted Pecan Spread

Simply elegant! This popular appetizer will be the toast of your next party.

**8 ounces cream cheese, softened**
**2 ounces blue cheese, crumbled**

**2 tablespoons toasted and coarsely chopped pecans**
**Pinch of kosher salt**
**Minced parsley**
**Baguette bread, sliced thinly**
**2 unpeeled Granny Smith apples, cored and sliced into eighths**
**2 unpeeled Macintosh apples, cored and sliced into eighths**
**Lemon juice**

Combine the first 4 ingredients and mix well. Place the mixture in a serving bowl and garnish with minced parsley. Serve immediately as a spread for the baguettes and apples. Or refrigerate and serve later. Before serving, dip the apple slices in fresh lemon juice to prevent browning.

*Makes 10 to 12 servings.*

## A Morehouse Moment

***Black Enterprise*** **magazine twice ranked Morehouse College as the number one college in the nation for educating African-American students. Morehouse, the nation's largest private, liberal arts college for African-American men, enrolls approximately 1,800 students annually. With an undergraduate enrollment of approximately 3,000 students, it confers bachelor's degrees on more black men than any other institution in the world. Morehouse offers a number of programs and activities to enhance its challenging liberal arts curriculum through the Leadership Center at Morehouse College, Morehouse Research Institute, and Andrew Young Center for International Affairs. According to Morehouse, it is one of only two historically black colleges or universities to produce three Rhodes scholars.**

# Blue Cheese Dip

**8 ounces cream cheese, softened**
**1/4 cup buttermilk**
**1 tablespoon sour cream**
**1/8 teaspoon garlic powder**
**4 ounces blue cheese, crumbled**

Process first 4 ingredients and half of the blue cheese until a smooth mixture forms. Stop occasionally to scrape down the sides. Stir in remaining blue cheese. Cover and chill 2 hours. Serve with vegetable crudités and apple or pear slices.

*Makes 3 cups.*

# Blue Cheese, Cranberry, Pine Nut, & Goat Cheese Spread

Inspired by cheese balls sold in Paris delis, this unique combination of ingredients will have you asking, *"Pouvez-vous dire délicieux?"* ("Can you say delicious?") Serve with toasted baguette slices.

**8 ounces goat cheese, softened**
**2 tablespoons Crème de Cassis liqueur**
**2 tablespoons dried cranberries**
**3/4 cup chopped toasted pine nuts**
**Baguette slices**

Blend or process the goat cheese and liqueur until it forms a smooth, creamy mixture. Chill for an hour before rolling the mixture into a smooth ball. Spread the cranberries and pine nuts on a plate. Roll the goat cheese ball in the cranberries and pine nuts. Chill for a minimum of two hours before serving. Serve at room temperature or chilled.

*Makes 6 servings.*

# Honeyed Sweet Potato Chips

Nothing says Southern cooking like sweet potatoes and honey roasted peanuts.

**1 cup honey roasted peanuts**
**Pinch of nutmeg**
**2 large sweet potatoes, sliced thin**
**10 tablespoons melted butter**
**Salt**

Preheat the oven to 475°F. Line 2 baking sheets with aluminum foil and grease well. Process the peanuts to a fine powder. Place the powder on a plate, add nutmeg, and mix well. Dip each potato slice into the butter until it is well coated. Coat both sides of each buttered potato slice with the peanut powder and arrange in a single layer on the prepared pans. Bake the potatoes for 12 to 18 minutes, or until they are tender and lightly browned. Make sure not to overcook as they will burn easily. Drain on paper towels, sprinkle with salt if desired, and serve warm.

*Makes 3 to 4 servings.*

# Jubilee Dip

**2 10-ounce bags frozen corn, thawed**
**2 14- to 16-ounce cans whole black beans, drained and rinsed**
**1 medium red onion, finely chopped**
**1 cup diced green bell pepper**
**1/2 cup diced red bell pepper**
**1 tablespoon parsley, finely chopped**
**1/4 cup sour cream**
**2 tablespoons red wine vinegar**
**1/2 cup mayonnaise**
**1 teaspoon ground cumin**

**1 teaspoon chili powder**
**Salt and pepper**

In a large bowl, combine corn, black beans, red onion, peppers, and parsley. In a small bowl, whisk together the sour cream, vinegar, mayonnaise, cumin, and chili powder until well combined. Toss dressing with corn and black bean mixture. Add salt and pepper to taste. Serve with corn chips.

*Makes 12 to 14 servings.*

## Julian Bond

**A student and social activist who faced jail for his convictions, and a U.S. legislator and black civil rights leader who fought to take his duly elected seat in the Georgia House of Representatives, Horace Julian Bond has remained on the cutting edge of social reform in**

Julian Bond, '71, student activist, member of the Georgia General Assembly for twenty years, and chairman of the NAACP.
*(Courtesy Morehouse College Archives)*

America since his days as a student protest leader at Morehouse College.

Born in 1940 to prominent educators, Bond began his career as a social activist at Morehouse, first as a founder of the Committee on Appeal for Human Rights (COAHR), a student civil rights organization that fought to integrate Atlanta's movie theaters, lunch counters, and parks; and then as a member of the Student Non-Violent Coordinating Committee, a protest powerhouse that forced states to enforce *Brown v. Board of Education* and pushed the federal government to enact more sweeping civil rights legislation.

Bond entered the political arena in 1965 after winning a one-year term to the Georgia House of Representatives, whose members refused to admit him because he had endorsed a SNCC statement accusing the United States of violating international law in Vietnam. He would be elected twice more before the Supreme Court unanimously ruled his exclusion unconstitutional. He was finally seated on January 9, 1967, and would hold his House seat for more than eight years. Bond also served as the first president of the Southern Poverty Law Center and chaired the national board of directors of the National Association for the Advancement of Colored People.

## A Morehouse Moment

At the Democratic National Convention in 1968, Julian Bond led a delegation of insurgents that won half the Georgia seats. He seconded the nomination of Eugene McCarthy and became the first black man to be nominated as the vice presidential candidate of a major party. He withdrew his name, however, because he was too young to meet the minimum age required under the Constitution.

**Dr. Martin Luther King, Jr., with student activists.**
*(Courtesy Morehouse College Archives)*

# Classic Clam Dip

Simply delicious and so easy that you will never purchase packaged clam dip again. Whip it up quickly when unexpected guests drop in, or up to two days in advance.

**2 6½-ounce cans of minced clams**
**8 ounces cream cheese, softened**
**¼ cup sour cream**
**¾ teaspoon Worcestershire sauce**
**2 tablespoons minced fresh parsley**
**2 garlic cloves, minced**
**Dash cayenne pepper**
**Freshly ground black pepper**

Drain the clams, reserving ¼ cup of juice. Beat the juice with the cream cheese, sour cream, and Worcestershire sauce. Fold in the clams, parsley, garlic, cayenne, and black pepper. Serve immediately or chill.

*Makes about 2 cups.*

**The Queen of Soul, Aretha Franklin, with student admirers in 1971.**
*(Courtesy Morehouse College Archives)*

# Layered Crab Dip

**2 8-ounce packages cream cheese, softened**
**2 tablespoons mayonnaise**
**1 tablespoon Old Bay seasoning**
**1½ cups fresh crab (claw meat), shredded**
**1 cup diced tomatoes**
**¼ cup sliced green onions**
**¼ cup (about 2 ounces) sliced black olives**

Combine the cream cheese, mayonnaise, and Old Bay seasoning in a medium-size bowl and mix thoroughly. Spread the cream cheese mixture evenly on the bottom of a 9-inch pie pan. Sprinkle crab meat, tomatoes, green onions, and black olives in layers over cream cheese mixture. Serve with tortilla chips and assorted crackers.

*Makes 16 servings.*

**Old School!**
*(Courtesy Morehouse College Archives)*

***"Morehouse is not in Atlanta, Georgia, alone but throughout the United States and the world wherever Morehouse men are found."***
**—Dr. Benjamin E. Mays**

# Spelman College

*Teach a woman and you teach a nation.*
—African Proverb

**Spelman Seminary faculty, 1890.**
*(Courtesy Spelman College Archives)*

***"I am building for a hundred years hence, not only for today."***

On April 11, 1881, Spelman, one of the nation's most highly regarded colleges for women, was founded in the basement of Friendship Baptist Church in Atlanta, Georgia, by Sophia B. Packard and Harriet "Hattie" E. Giles. The two friends, who often dressed alike, "had made a compact to enter jointly upon the profession of teaching and as soon as practicable establish a school of their own." In 1879 Packard was commissioned by the Woman's American Baptist Home Mission Society (WABHMS), which she had helped to found, to study the living conditions "among the freedmen of the South." As an educator and administrator of several outstanding New England Academies, she was especially concerned with the lack of educational opportunities for black women. While in New Orleans, she became ill and

**Harriet Giles** ***(left)*** **and Sophia Packard** ***(right)***
*(Courtesy Spelman College Archives)*

sent for Giles to assist her. Giles was equally appalled by the circumstances of Southern blacks, especially women, and the pair returned to Boston convinced that they were called by God to establish a school for the education and elevation of black women in the South.

Miss Packard and Miss Giles reached Atlanta on April 1, 1881, and were met at the depot by Dr. Shaver, a teacher at the Atlanta Baptist Seminary. The next day, after locating accommodations, they were introduced to Reverend Frank Quarles. With a congregation of 1500, he was one of the most influential black preachers in the city. Upon explaining their mission to him, Reverend Quarles exclaimed, "When I was praying, the Lord heard and answered. I was on my knees pleading with God to send teachers for the Baptist women and girls of Georgia. We fully believe the Lord sent you."

Following a meeting of the local clergy in Reverend Quarles's study, which was called by Packard and Giles "to consider what steps should be taken to promote the education of the young ladies connected with your congregation," one week later, on April 11, 1881, the first class convened in the basement of Friendship Baptist Church.

Packard and Giles carried the banner for more room and better facilities north. In Cleveland they met John D. Rockefeller, who pledged 250 dollars toward the building fund. He told them, "You know, there are so many who come here and get us to give money. Then they're gone, and we don't know where they are—where their work is. Do you mean to stick? If you do, you'll hear from me again."

So began what was later described as the year of miracles. In June 1882, a group of several black ministers, including William Jefferson White, one of the three founders of Morehouse College, organized the Baptist Educational Society to establish a building fund for the school. Each member contributed five cents a month to the fund and the students were encouraged to recruit members. In less than three months 25 dollars was raised, representing the first fund-raising effort by students.

In February 1883, the school relocated to its new nine-acre site, which included five frame buildings with both classroom and residence hall space.

A model school was opened and served a dual purpose. It provided practical experience for those pursuing a teaching career while also providing an elementary education to younger students, many of whom would later attend the Seminary School.

During this period, Dr. Morehouse and the American Baptist Home

**Giles Hall, named for Harriet E. Giles.**
*(Archives and Special Collections: Robert Woodruff Library at the Atlanta University Center)*

**Howe Hall Chapel Service, ca. 1887.**
*(Courtesy Spelman College Archives)*

Mission felt that the society could not afford to pay for separate properties for men and women and hoped to consolidate the Seminary School with the Atlanta Baptist Seminary. However, he told Packard that the new site could be devoted to the exclusive use of the women's school if they would take over the mortgage. Teachers volunteered their services, and gifts of furnishings, supplies, and clothing were sent from the North, but despite these contributions and cost-saving measures, in April 1884, on the third anniversary of its founding, the school found itself in dire straits.

During these darkest of days John D. Rockefeller arrived unannounced with Mrs. Rockefeller, her sister, and her mother, Mrs. Lucy Henry Spelman. Rockefeller was so impressed with the seminary that in yet another miraculous act, he settled the debt on the property. At Packard's suggestion to its governing boards, the school's name was changed to Spelman Seminary in honor and recognition of the Spelman family's longtime activism in the antislavery movement. The home of Mr. and Mrs. Buel Spelman had served as a station on the underground railroad for slaves on their journey north in search of freedom. At the school's three-year anniversary Mrs. Spelman would recall that the only meals she ever prepared on the Sabbath were for slaves journeying northward.

As a result of their hard work and prayer, another milestone in the school's history was reached in 1887 when diplomas were given to the first six women to complete the Higher Normal and Scientific Course.

Even as Spelman progressed toward becoming a women's college, it continued to offer an industrial curriculum in an attempt to make education practical. Included in the department offerings were sewing, millinery, housekeeping, laundering, printing, and cooking. By 1901 Miss Giles could boast, "Certificates are given on the successful completion of a course in cooking which covers three years, with one lesson of an hour and a half each week. The equipment is good. In a large room there are sixteen sets of individual cooking outfits and eight small gas stoves. . . . "

**Spelman High School graduates, 1887.**
*(Courtesy Spelman College Archives)*

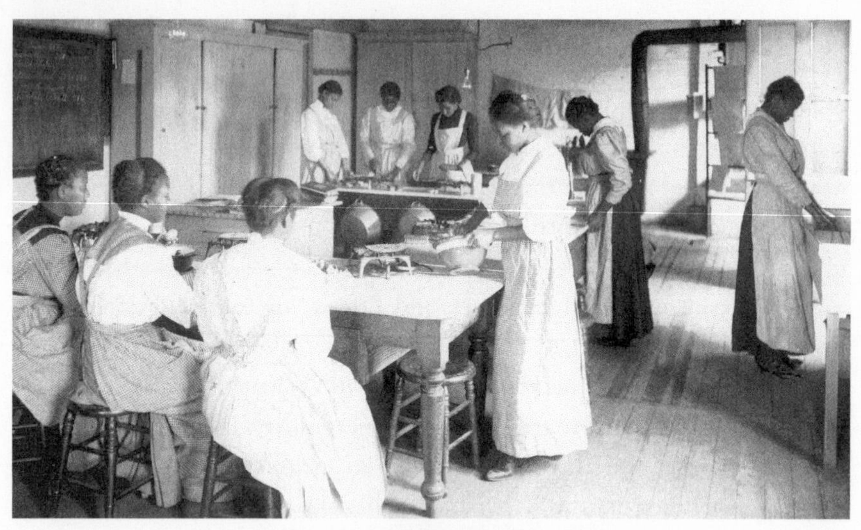

**Students in cooking class, ca. 1890.**
*(Courtesy Spelman College Archives)*

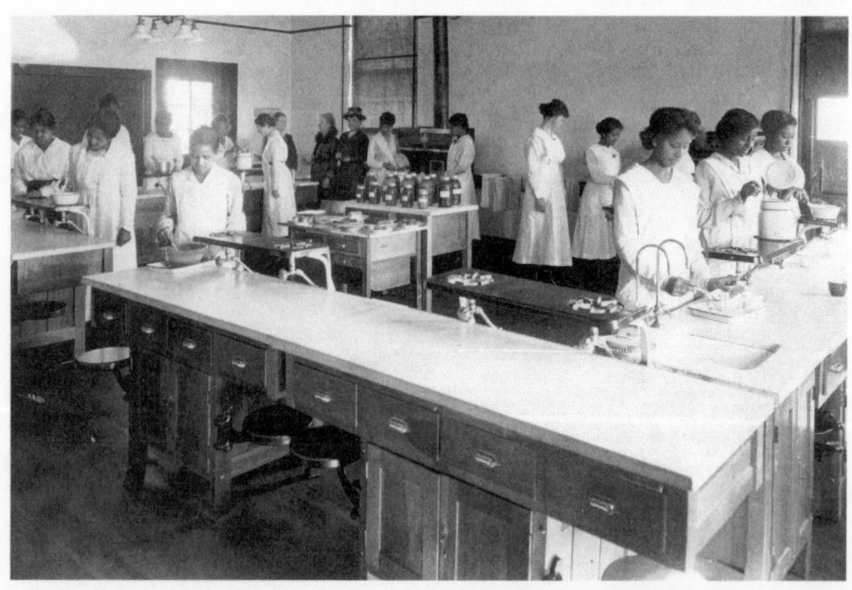

**Cooking class in Laura Spelman Hall, ca. 1917.**
*(Courtesy Spelman College Archives)*

During the school's early years the cooking classes, in addition to educating students, also prepared the students' meals. Staples such as flour and sugar were ordered from Atlanta. However, white delivery men refused to deliver them to the buildings. Instead, they threw them over the fence, forcing students and teachers to carry them to the kitchen.

In the kitchen students turned the offensive acts into sweet delight by creating delectable treats such as the following Ginger Cookies and Mother's Cake.

### Recipes from the Spelman Cooking School

## Ginger Cookies

**1 cup shortening**
**1 cup sugar**
**2 eggs, well beaten**
**1 cup molasses**
**1 cup sour milk**
**2 teaspoons ginger**
**1 teaspoon cinnamon**
**2 teaspoons soda**
**1/2 teaspoon salt**
**Flour to roll**

Cream the shortening, add the sugar and the eggs and beat well, then add the molasses and milk. Sift the spice, soda, and salt with three cups of the flour, add to the first mixture, and then add just enough more flour so that a small quantity can be handled at a time, on a well floured board. Do not roll too thin. Cut out and place some distance apart on a greased pan. Bake in a moderate oven.

# Mother's Cake

**3/4 cup butter**
**1 1/2 cups sugar**
**3 eggs, beaten separately**
**1 teaspoon lemon or vanilla extract**
**1 teaspoon mace**
**2/3 cup milk**
**3 cups flour**
**4 teaspoons baking powder**

Cream the butter, add the sugar gradually, then yolks of eggs and flavoring [extract]. Sift the mace, flour and baking powder and add alternately with the milk a little at a time, and then the stiffly beaten whites. Beat thoroughly.

If baked in a loaf it will require nearly an hour in a moderate oven. If baked in layers, about 20 minutes.

This cake may be varied by adding a cup of chopped nuts or raisins, or half a cup of chopped dates.

When Frankie Quarles was first presented by her mother, an alum of the school and the widow of Reverend Frank Quarles, Miss Packard, perhaps in remembrance of all the Quarles family had done for them, refused to "receive a dollar for her education." From that root of loyal friendship and academic excellence, five generations of Spelman women would grow and experience the leadership of strongly committed Spelman presidents. Among them were leaders for a new era such as Lucy Hale Tapley.

Before being elected to the presidency in March of 1910, Lucy Hale Tapley worked with the founders for twenty years. As president she specifically adopted Miss Packard's five aims for Spelman students:

> To train the intellect, to store the mind with useful knowledge, to induce habits of industry and desire for general information, to inspire a love for the true and the beautiful, to prepare the pupils for the practical duties of life—the hallmark of a liberal education.

**Frankie Quarles**
*(Courtesy Spelman College Archives)*

**Graduating class, 1910.**
*(Courtesy Spelman College Archives)*

Florence Read *(left)* and Lucy Tapley *(right)*
*(Courtesy Spelman College Archives)*

Spelman campus, ca. 1910.
*(Courtesy Spelman College Archives)*

During this period Spelman began moving toward its destiny as an institution of higher education for African-American women. Students pursuing a liberal arts education would receive degrees, while those majoring in secondary education and home economics education received diplomas, striking a balance between those seeking an academic education and Tapley's desire to see the school produce teachers as a means of bettering communities. On June 1, 1924, the name was officially changed to Spelman College.

# Beverages

**Spelman College's earliest students had a thirst that only knowledge could satisfy and endured much to obtain it. We hope the following recipes, including perennial favorites such as lemonade and sweet tea will slake your thirst. Many are old time Southern favorites. Some celebrate the bounties of the South with a new twist, such as fresh peach lemonade, peach nectar in a Mason jar and watermelon lemonade. Other recipes, such as Jamaican hibiscus drink, give a nod of appreciation to those from other cultures who settled in Atlanta, contributing to its growth and attending its fine institutions of higher learning while adding their own recipes to the evolving culinary experience that enriches this exciting Southern city.**

## Fresh Peach Lemonade

Georgia peaches never tasted so good! This delicious drink, which celebrates the marriage of Georgia peaches and Southern lemonade, produces a wonderfully unique beverage.

**3 peaches, peeled and chopped**
**1 1/2 cups granulated sugar**
**4 cups water**
**1 cup freshly squeezed lemon juice**
**Peach slices**
**Mint sprigs**

Combine the peaches, sugar, and water in a saucepan; mix well and bring to a boil over medium-high heat. Reduce heat and allow mixture to simmer until the sugar dissolves, approximately 10 minutes. Remove from heat and cool before straining into a large pitcher by pressing through a sieve to extract as much juice as possible.

Stir in the lemon juice, adjust flavor to taste, chill, and serve in tall, ice-filled glasses. Garnish each glass with a peach slice and a mint sprig.

*Makes 8 servings.*

# Peach Nectar Lemonade

Peach nectar is a sweet contrast to the pucker-up tartness of lemons, and it provides a new twist to this summertime favorite.

**2 cups water**
**3/4 cup sugar**
**4 12-ounce cans peach nectar**
**3/4 cup fresh lemonade**
**Spearmint sprigs for garnish**
**Rock candy stirrer**

In a saucepan combine the water and sugar, bring the mixture to a boil over medium-high heat, stirring until the sugar dissolves. Reduce the heat and simmer for an additional 5 minutes. Allow the mixture to cool, pour into a serving pitcher, and refrigerate to chill. Stir in the remaining ingredients and pour into tall, freezer frosted, ice-filled glasses. Garnish with a fresh sprig of mint. To frost glasses, set them on a tray in the freezer compartment until covered with frost. For an even more delightful presentation, dip the rims in tinted sugar and fill with beverage or return unfilled glasses to the sugar to set properly. Throw in a matching rock candy stirrer for a little added pizzaz. Go ahead, you've got plenty!

*Makes 4 servings.*

# Peach Nectar in a Mason Jar

If you have plenty, a Mason jar is as acceptable as Waterford crystal when the offering is as delicious and refreshing as this one.

**3 12-ounce cans peach nectar**
**1/3 cup sugar**
**1/2 cup fresh lemonade**
**1 quart carbonated lemon-lime soda**

Combine the first three ingredients in a two-quart serving pitcher. Mix well until the sugar dissolves and refrigerate to chill. Just before serving, add the carbonated lemon soda. Stir well and pour into tall, ice-filled Mason jars.

*Makes 4 to 6 servings.*

# Watermelon Lemonade

**8 cups watermelon, cubed and seeded**
**1/2 cup raspberries**
**1/4 cup water**
**1/2 cup sugar**
**3/4 cup fresh lemon juice**
**1/4 cup pineapple juice**

Process the watermelon, raspberries, and water in a food processor until they are blended smooth. Strain the mixture through a fine mesh strainer into a serving pitcher. Stir in sugar, lemon juice, and pineapple juice until sugar dissolves. Refrigerate until thoroughly chilled, approximately 1 hour. Serve in tall, chilled, ice-filled glasses.

*Makes 4 to 6 servings.*

# Blueberry Lemonade

Matchless!

**5 cups water, divided**
**$1^1/_4$ to $1^1/_2$ cups sugar, or to taste, divided**
**Zest and juice from 6 large lemons**
**$1^1/_4$ cups fresh blueberries**

In a medium saucepan, combine 2 cups of the water with $1^1/_4$ cups of the sugar and bring to a boil over medium heat, stirring until the sugar dissolves and forms syrup. Increase the heat to medium-high and cook an additional 5 minutes, or until the syrup begins to thicken slightly. Stir in the remaining 3 cups of water, lemon zest, and juice; remove from heat and set aside.

Purée the berries and add them to the syrup. Allow the mixture to cool at room temperature for at least 1 hour. Adjust taste with the remaining sugar, and strain the lemonade into a large pitcher to remove the seeds and skins. Chill until ready to serve. Pour into tall, ice-filled glasses.

*Makes 4 to 6 servings.*

**Students in sewing class, ca. 1920.**
*(Courtesy Spelman College Archives)*

# Pineapple Lemon-Limeade

Surprise your guests with this classically tasty, yet unique lemon-limeade!

**2 cups sugar**
**2 cups water**
**2 cups unsweetened pineapple juice**
**2 cups seltzer or sparkling water**
**1/2 cup fresh lemon juice**
**1/2 cup lime juice**
**5 lemon slices**
**5 lime slices**
**8 mint sprigs**

Combine sugar with water and bring to a boil over medium-high heat. Stir until sugar dissolves, reduce heat and allow mixture to simmer undisturbed for 10 minutes. Cool syrup to room temperature and stir in pineapple juice, seltzer, and remaining juices. Pour into tall, ice-filled glasses. Garnish with lemon and lime slices and mint sprigs.

*Makes 6 servings.*

# Cranberry Pink Lemonade

Pretty in pink!

**2 cups white sugar**
**9 cups water**
**2 cups fresh lemon juice**
**1 cup cranberry juice, chilled**

Combine the above ingredients in a large pitcher. Stir mixture until the sugar dissolves and refrigerate to chill. Pour into tall, ice-filled glasses and garnish with fresh mint.

*Makes 12 servings.*

# Georgia Peach Tea

This refreshing tea is a delicious reminder that Georgia is the peach tree state!

**4 11 1/2-ounce cans peach nectar**
**2 1/2 quarts brewed tea, chilled**
**1 1/4 cups sugar**
**1/4 cup lemon juice**

Combine the above ingredients, mix well, and refrigerate to chill. Serve in tall, chilled, ice filled-glasses.

*Makes approximately 1 gallon (10 servings).*

**Students in benchwork class, ca. 1890.**
*(Courtesy Spelman College Archives)*

# Sweet Georgia Peach Iced Tea

Sweet, sweet Georgia peach tea. Peaches are the golden child of summer, and this refreshing drink is the liquid gold standard of Southern hospitality.

**8 cups boiling water**
**8 tea bags**
**1-inch cinnamon stick**
**1 cup sugar**
**48 ounces peach nectar**
**2 1/2 cups cold water**
**Fresh peach slices (choose one or two that are slightly under-ripe and firm)**
**Fresh basil to garnish**

In a large heat-proof container, pour boiling water over the tea bags and cinnamon stick; steep for 5 minutes. Remove and discard the tea bags. Refrigerate the tea to chill. Before serving, add the sugar, nectar, and water; mix well until the sugar dissolves. Transfer the tea to a serving pitcher, and pour into ice-filled glasses. Garnish with a fresh Georgia peach slice and a sprig of basil.

*Makes 8 to 10 servings.*

**Sisters Chapel**
*(Courtesy Spelman College Archives)*

*"When you enter Sisters Chapel, you immediately feel the spirit of hundreds of thousands of people who have gathered here for over seventy-five years for various occasions. Something there is about Sisters Chapel that blurs lines that separate our lives into the past, the present and the future. Something there is about Sisters Chapel that gives us clarity about the present, appreciation for the past, and direction for the future. Something there is about Sisters Chapel that makes it a place in which memories resound with harmony."*

**—Author unknown**

# Summertime Tea

Summer living is definitely easy with this cool invigorating tea. Try this Southern summertime classic for a jubilantly refreshing celebration of the season. Enjoy!

**5 cups water**
**2½ cups pineapple juice**
**1 cup fresh orange juice**
**½ cup granulated sugar or to taste**
**½ teaspoon ground cinnamon**
**¼ teaspoon ground cloves**
**5 tea bags (black, orange pekoe)**

Bring water to a boil over medium-high heat; stir in juices, sugar, and spices. Bring to a second boil; reduce heat and simmer until the sugar dissolves. Remove saucepan from heat and add tea bags. Steep the tea for 4 to 5 minutes. Remove and discard the tea bags and allow mixture to cool to room temperature before refrigerating to chill. Serve over ice in 4 tall, chilled, ice-filled glasses.

*Makes 4 servings.*

**Students in chemistry class, ca. 1890.**
*(Courtesy Spelman College Archives)*

# Tropical Fruit Tea

Relive your escape to the tropics with every tasty sip.

**1 10-ounce package frozen raspberries, thawed**
**3 cups water**
**1/3 cup sugar**
**1 family size tea bag**
**2 cups red grape juice**
**1/4 cup lime juice**
**1 lemon, sliced**
**1 lime, sliced**
**1 orange, sliced thin**
**7 strawberries, hulled and sliced thin**
**1 16-ounce bottle sparkling orange drink, chilled**

Purée raspberries and press through a fine wire-mesh strainer into a large container, discarding remaining pulp. Set puréed mixture aside and bring water and sugar to a boil over medium-high heat, stirring often to prevent scorching. Remove from heat and add the tea bag. Cover and steep 5 minutes. Remove the tea bag with a slotted spoon, squeezing gently. Allow the tea mixture to cool. Combine the tea mixture with the remaining ingredients except orange drink; mix well and chill. Add orange soda immediately before serving in tall, ice-filled, chilled glasses.

*Makes 8 to 10 servings.*

# Summer Hibiscus Tea Cooler

Reminiscent of the rose-colored iced drinks served during Caribbean street carnivals, this tea is best made 12 to 24 hours before serving.

**8 tea bags (choose Red Zinger or any other tea containing hibiscus flowers)**
**1 cinnamon stick**
**4 cups boiling water**
**1 quart chilled pineapple juice**
**1 quart chilled sparkling water**
**1½ cups orange juice**
**1 tablespoon fresh squeezed lemon juice**
**Orange slices for garnish**

Add tea bags and cinnamon stick to the boiling water and steep 30 minutes. Remove and discard the tea bags and cinnamon stick; refrigerate the tea for approximately 12 hours or overnight.

Combine the tea with the pineapple juice, sparkling water, orange juice, and lemon juice. Stir. Adjust flavor to taste by adding additional water and/or sugar. Serve over ice in tall, chilled glasses and garnish with orange slices.

*Makes 18 servings.*

# Jamaican Hibiscus Drink

**8 cups water**
**2 cups dried hibiscus blossoms (sometimes called sorrel blossoms, they can be found in Jamaican or Mexican markets)**
**1¼ teaspoons grated fresh ginger**
**1¼ cups sugar, or to taste**
**Jamaican rum to taste (optional)**

Bring water to boil in a 4-quart stainless steel or other non-reactive pot. Add the hibiscus and ginger. Remove from heat; cover and steep for 4 hours before straining and sweetening to taste. Chill and serve just as it is or add very good rum, according to your taste.

*Makes 2 quarts.*

# Cranberry Tea

Equally enjoyable year-round and a surprising eye-opener, this tangy cranberry drink is a great accompaniment to Thanksgiving dinner—or great heated as a winter drink.

**1 gallon water**
**1 cup granulated sugar**
**15 tea bags**
**1 12-ounce can frozen cranberry juice concentrate, partially thawed and undiluted**
**2 cups orange juice**
**2 tablespoons lime juice**

**Spelman and Morehouse baccalaureate service, 1928.**
*(Courtesy Spelman College Archives)*

Bring water to a boil; add sugar and stir until dissolved. Add tea bags and steep 4 to 5 minutes, or to taste. Stir in juices and allow the tea to cool at room temperature before refrigerating. Serve in six tall, ice-filled glasses.

*Makes 6 servings.*

# Watermelon Punch in a Watermelon Shell

Cool, ruby red slices of watermelon set in dew-kissed emerald shells are almost emblematic of summer. It's a shame to just eat them when they also make delicious drinks. When selecting a melon look for one that feels heavy for its size. The rind should be bright green, without bruises, dents or cuts, with a cream-colored or buttery yellow underside. The stem should be green and fresh looking. And finally, it should produce a resonant sound, not a dull thud, when thumped.

**1 large watermelon**
**1 3/4 cups sugar**
**1 1/4 cups water**
**1 tablespoon fresh lime juice**
**1 33.8-ounce bottle sparkling lemon-lime drink**
**Fresh mint leaves (optional)**

Cut a thin slice of melon from the bottom (buttery yellow side) of the melon, just enough to stabilize it when you turn it over. Turn melon over. It should sit flat on the table or counter without rolling or tilting. Slice the top 1/3 of the melon away. The pink flesh should be exposed with sufficient shell left to form a bowl once the pulp has been scooped from it.

Scoop pulp from the melon, remove the seeds, and mash the pulp. Measure 1 gallon of juice from the pulp and set aside. Next, use a paring knife to scallop or make other decorations to the edge of the watermelon shell.

Combine sugar, water, and lime juice in a saucepan; bring the mixture to a boil over medium-high, reduce heat, and simmer 5 minutes. Add the mixture to the reserved watermelon juice and chill. Before serving, add the lemon-lime drink and mix gently. Pour the punch into the watermelon shell and sprinkle the top with 5 to 7 fresh mint leaves.

*Makes 18 ½-cup servings.*

# Golden Peach Nectar Punch

As light and refreshing as morning dew, this sweet nectar is absolutely delectable.

**2 liters lemon-lime soda**
**2 quarts peach nectar**
**2 quarts pineapple juice**
**½ cup lemon juice**

Combine the above ingredients. Mix well and pour into an ice-filled punch bowl just before serving.

*Makes 24 servings.*

# Legacy & Lace: A Lavender Tea Punch

**2 cups water**
**⅔ cup sugar**
**3 tablespoons snipped fresh mint**
**1 large stem of unsprayed fresh lavender**
**½ cup orange juice**
**1 cup pineapple juice**
**¼ cup lemon juice**

**2 cups strong brewed tea**
**1 1-liter bottle club soda, chilled**

Combine the water, sugar, mint, and lavender in a large stainless-steel or non-reactive pan. Bring the mixture to a rapid boil over medium-high heat before removing from heat and allowing it to steep for 20 minutes. Next, strain mixture through a cotton cheesecloth-lined colander.

Add the juices and tea to the lavender infused water and chill. Immediately before serving add the club soda.

*Makes 16 servings.*

## A Summer Reunion Fruit Punch for Fifty

As refreshing as it is delicious! And remember this tip: When planning your event, count on 350 cubes of ice for 50 people, or seven per person.

**3½ cups sugar**
**1 pint hot tea**
**2 cups fresh lemon juice**
**3 quarts orange juice**
**1 quart pineapple juice**
**3 quarts ice water**
**1 quart ginger ale**
**1 cup sliced strawberries**
**1 cup pineapple chunks with juice**
**1 cup sliced white grapes**

Combine the above ingredients and mix well. Store in batches in the refrigerator until needed to fill or refill the punch bowl. To serve, pour into ice-filled punch bowl.

*Makes 50 servings.*

Commencement reception, 1961.
*(Courtesy Spelman College Archives)*

## Marian Wright Edelman, Spelman '60

*"Education remains one of the black community's most enduring values. It is sustained by the belief that freedom and education go hand in hand. . . . "*

—Marian Wright Edelman in *Black America,* 1989

*"When I was sitting where you are, we were getting thrown out of the gallery of the legislature where Julian Bond, Grace Hamilton, and others sit today. We were going to jail. . . . We were picketing Rich's and Davison's, whose lunch counters and jobs were closed to us even with a Spelman degree."*

—Marian Wright Edelman, in a 1980 speech to the graduating class of Spelman

Marian Wright Edelman, founder and president of the Children's Defense Fund, was the youngest of five children and credits her Baptist preacher father with instilling in her an obligation to right wrongs. When African Americans in her hometown were not allowed to enter city parks, her father built a park for African-American children behind his church.

Edelman is a graduate of Spelman College and Yale Law School. As director of the NAACP Legal Defense and Education Fund office in Jackson, Mississippi, she became the first African-American female admitted to the Mississippi bar. She also was nationally recognized as an advocate for Head Start at this time. In 1968, Edelman moved to Washington, D.C., and became counsel to the Poor People's Campaign organized by Dr. Martin Luther King, Jr. She founded the Washington Research Project, where she lobbied Congress for child and family nutrition programs and expanding Head Start. In 1973, the Washington Research Project became the Children's Defense Fund (CDF), the United States' leading advocacy group for children. As president of the CDF, Edelman has worked to decrease teenage pregnancy, increase Medicaid coverage for poor children, and secure government funding for programs like Head Start.

Edelman has served as director of the Center for Law and Edu-

Marian Wright with Charles Merrill, 1959.
*(Courtesy Spelman College Archives)*

**cation at Harvard and is the first African-American female on the board of Yale. Her publications include *The Measure of Our Success: A Letter to My Children and Yours.* Edelman's awards include the Albert Schweitzer Humanitarian Prize, the Heinz Award, the Ella J. Baker Prize, the MacArthur Foundation Fellowship Prize, and the Presidential Medal of Freedom, the nation's highest civilian award.**

***"Service is a rent you pay for living."***
**—Marian Wright Edelman**

# Pineapple Punch

This is a wonderful punch to serve to younger children because, when spilled, it is less likely to stain than other fruit punches. When serving it to the very youngest partygoers, however, omit the cherries; toddlers or other young children may choke on them.

**1 46-ounce can pineapple juice**
**1 liter lemon-lime soda**
**10 ounces Maraschino cherries with juice (optional)**

Combine the above chilled ingredients in a bowl, mix well, and add ice. While not necessary, chilling your punch ingredients before serving permits the use of less ice to chill the punch and also slows its melting time, making for a less watery punch.

*Makes 30 servings.*

# White Grape Pineapple Punch

As delicious as it is lovely!

**1 16-ounce can white grape juice**
**2 12-ounce cans pineapple juice concentrate**
**1 6-ounce can frozen lemonade juice concentrate**
**1/4 cup lime juice**
**Ice**

Combine grape juice, pineapple juice, lemonade concentrate, and lime juice in a punch bowl. Mix well until concentrate is thoroughly blended. Add ice and mix well to chill at least 15 minutes before serving, allowing the ice to dilute the fruit concentrates. Add water to taste, if necessary, just before serving.

*Makes 24 servings.*

## Ruby Doris Smith Robinson

*"The civil rights movement of the 1950s and 1960s was largely carried by women whose organizing skills and political consciousness evolved from years of unflagging involvement in social change. The success of the Black freedom struggle was a result of the courageous leadership and selfless commitment of women who dedicated their lives to the vision of a free and just society."*

—Ella Baker, civil rights activist

Ruby Doris Smith
*(Courtesy Spelman College Archives)*

One of those women who dedicated her life to the cause was Ruby Doris Smith Robinson. She was born in Atlanta, Georgia, on April 25, 1942, to Reverend and Mrs. James Smith. Upon being accepted by Spelman College, she became a member of another community of women and heir to a legacy of social activism in action.

*"By the spring of 1960, Ruby Doris was caught in a struggle which would change the world forever—the civil rights movement. As a freshwoman at Spelman College, Ruby—along with Julian Bond and others—organized the Atlanta Committee on Appeal for Human Rights. She was one of the original freedom riders in Jackson, Mississippi. In 1963 Ruby Doris withdrew from Spelman and devoted full time service to S.N.C.C. Like many other sisters of all kinds, Ruby Doris managed to maintain a very active role in the civil rights movement while continuing her education and maintaining her family life. Returning to Spelman in 1964, she completed a bachelor of science degree. Ruby Doris died of a rare cancer on October 7, 1967, at the age of 25. A news release from S.N.C.C. said this: 'During her 7 years in the movement, she was the heart of S.N.C.C. as well as one of the committee's dedicated administrators. . . . ' Now there are many 'sheroes' of the Civil Rights Movement . . . But none stands out more for me than a Spelman student. Her name: Ruby Doris Smith . . . We must never forget her story."*

—Dr. Johnetta Cole at the fifth meeting of President's Commission on the Celebration of Women in American History, held on January 15, 1999, at the Martin Luther King, Jr. Center in Atlanta, Georgia

All gave some. Some gave all!

# Festive Cranberry Punch

A lovely holiday punch; it is chilled by the fruit concentrates without being diluted by melting ice.

**64 ounces cranberry juice**
**1 quart pineapple juice**
**1 cup granulated sugar**
**1 quart carbonated lemon-lime soda**

Combine cranberry juice, pineapple juice, and sugar. Stir mixture until sugar dissolves and freeze. Prior to serving, thaw juice in covered punch bowl until it forms a solid slush, approximately 1 hour. Add soda just prior to serving, mix well.

*Makes 36 servings.*

# Everything Raspberry Punch

**2 12-ounce cans frozen concentrated raspberry-kiwi juice, partially thawed**
**2 2-liter bottles raspberry crème soda, chilled**
**1 gallon raspberry sherbet**
**Fresh raspberries, washed**

Combine raspberry-kiwi juice concentrate and raspberry soda in a large punch bowl. Use an ice cream scoop to gently add large scoops of sherbet to the mixture. Add ice to taste or as necessary to keep mixture chilled. Garnish with fresh raspberries just before serving.

*Makes 48 servings.*

# Simply Fruit Punch

**1 46-ounce can pineapple juice, chilled**
**1 46-ounce can apricot nectar, chilled**
**1 6-ounce can frozen limeade concentrate**
**2 liters lemon-lime soda, chilled**
**10 ounces maraschino cherries with juice, chilled**

Combine the above chilled ingredients in bowl; mix well and add ice. While not necessary, chilling your punch ingredients before serving permits the use of less ice to chill the punch and also causes the ice to melt more slowly, making for a less watery punch.

*Makes 30 servings.*

# Tropical Island Punch

**1 64-ounce bottle fruit punch, chilled**
**2 15-ounce cans pineapple chunks, chilled**
**1 pint strawberries, stemmed, hulled, and sliced**
**2 bananas, sliced**
**2 pints lemon sherbet**
**1 2-liter bottle lemon-lime soda**
**Ice**

Pour fruit punch into a large bowl, add fruit, scoops of the sherbet, and slowly pour soda over the mixture. Add ice to taste or as necessary.

*Makes 30 servings.*

# Spiked Fruit Punch

**2 16-ounce cans frozen pineapple juice concentrate**
**12 ounces spiced rum**
**2 2-liter bottles lemon-lime soda, chilled**
**1 10-ounce jar maraschino cherries, chilled**
**4 oranges, sliced into rounds**
**2 trays frozen pineapple juice cubes**

Combine pineapple juice concentrate and rum in a large punch bowl. Add lemon-lime soda and maraschino cherry juice; stir to combine. Float cherries and orange slices on top. Add frozen pineapple cubes before serving.

*Makes 48 servings.*

# A Georgia Peach Champagne Punch

**4 11 1/2-ounce cans peach nectar**
**1 6-ounce can frozen orange juice concentrate**
**1/4 cup lemon juice**
**1 tablespoon lime juice**
**1/2 cup peach brandy**
**1/4 cup grenadine syrup**
**4 750-milliliter bottles champagne**

Chill all ingredients before using them. In a large punch bowl combine peach nectar, concentrated orange juice, lemon juice, lime juice, brandy, and grenadine. Mix well and add champagne. Serve immediately.

*Makes 24 servings.*

# Strawberry Champagne Punch

Perfect for a bridal shower or other special event.

**1 750-milliliter bottle champagne, chilled**
**2 liters ginger ale, chilled**
**1 10-ounce package frozen strawberries, thawed and puréed**
**1 pint fresh strawberries, washed, stemmed, hulled, and sliced**

In a large punch bowl, combine champagne, ginger ale, and strawberry purée. Stir gently, add the fresh strawberry slices, and serve immediately.

*Makes 14 servings.*

## Alice Walker

**Alice Walker, one of the leading voices among black American women writers, attended Spelman from 1961 to 1963 before transferring to Sarah Lawrence College. By age 38 she had produced a large body of work, critically acclaimed for its frank and insightful portrayal of the black cultural experience in America and that of black women in particular. Her most famous work, *The Color Purple,* portrays the lives of Southern black women as they overcome sexism and racism through nurturing and empowering female friendships. The winner of both the Pulitzer Prize and the American Book Award, *The Color Purple* was made into a popular motion picture that received several Academy Award nominations and a Broadway musical. Her books have been translated into more than two dozen languages.**

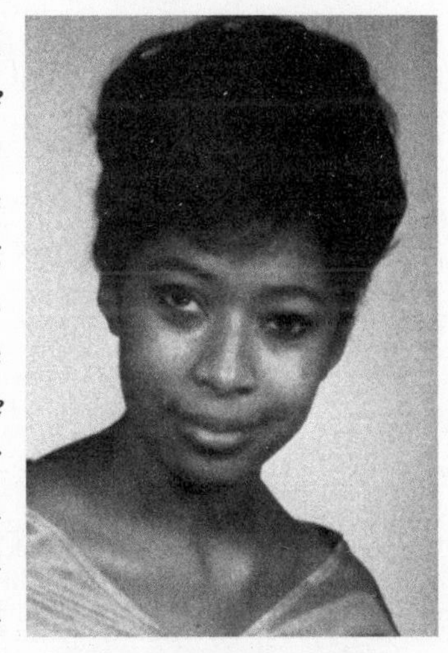

Alice Walker, ca. 1964.
*(Courtesy Spelman College Archives)*

**The youngest of eight children born to impoverished Southern sharecroppers in Eatonville, Georgia, Walker was especially influenced by her parents' storytelling, especially that of her mother, whom she described as "a walking history of our community." Perhaps as a reflection of Walker's view of her mother as a community griot, the preservation of black culture through strong black female characters is a dominant theme in her work.**

# Daiquiri Punch

The thirst-quenching, fresh, delicious flavor of this punch makes all the added effort very much worthwhile. If you don't have an electric juicer or access to free labor (family and friends), plan ahead, juice in increments, and freeze.

**2 quarts fresh lemon juice**
**4 quarts fresh lime juice**
**4 quarts orange juice**
**1 pound confectioners' sugar**
**4 quarts club soda**
**2½ fifths light rum**

Combine the fruit juices and confectioners' sugar and mix well; refrigerate to chill for several hours. Add club soda and rum just before serving in tall glasses, filled with cracked ice and garnished with fresh mint.

*Makes 75 servings.*

# Whiskey Sour Punch

This is a wonderful punch to serve at events ranging from weddings to barbecues. Remember this tip: Your ice will melt away slower if you make large cubes in muffin cups.

**1 quart lemon juice**
**1 quart orange juice**
**1 quart whiskey**
**3 quarts sparkling water**
**Sugar to taste**

Combine the above ingredients; pour over large cubes or a block of ice and garnish with slivers of fresh pineapple.

*Makes 50 servings.*

## Piña Colada Punch

**3 cups well-blended cream of coconut, chilled**
**7 1/2 cups unsweetened pineapple juice, chilled**
**4 1/2 cups light rum**
**5 trays frozen pineapple juice cubes**

Blend together the cream of coconut, pineapple juice, and rum in batches. Transfer to a large punch bowl and add frozen pineapple cubes just before serving.

*Makes 24 servings.*

## Wedding Punch

**2 12-ounce cans frozen lemonade concentrate**
**2 12-ounce cans frozen pineapple juice concentrate**
**2 quarts lemon-lime soda, chilled**
**Up to 2 bottles champagne, chilled**
**Fresh strawberries**
**Mint leaves**

Combine juices and 1 quart of the lemon-lime soda in a large punch bowl; mix well. Immediately before serving, add remaining lemon-lime soda, ginger ale, and champagne to taste. Stir to blend. Garnish with strawberries and a sprig of mint.

*Makes 30 servings.*

## Red Velvet Punch

**8 cups cranberry juice cocktail**
**2 cups brandy**
**1 6-ounce can frozen orange juice concentrate, thawed**
**1 6-ounce can frozen pineapple juice concentrate, thawed**
**1 6-ounce can frozen lime juice concentrate, thawed**
**2 fifths chilled champagne**
**Lemon and/or lime slices**

Mix cranberry juice cocktail, brandy, orange juice, pineapple juice, and lime juice in a large punch bowl over a block of ice. Just before serving, add chilled champagne. Garnish with slices of lemon and/or lime.

*Makes 25 servings, allowing 3 cups per guest.*

*Note:* For non-alcoholic punch, substitute 2 quarts of ginger ale for the champagne and 2 cups of grape juice for the brandy.

## Cosmopolitan Punch

Smooth and urbane, this punch is definitely not for kids, but it may make you giggle like one.

**60 ounces or 40 1½-ounce jiggers vodka**
**2½ cups Cointreau**
**¾ cup + 2 tablespoons fresh lime juice**
**8 cups cranberry juice**

**1 10-ounce jar maraschino cherries and juice**
**1 2-liter bottle lemon-lime soda, chilled**

Combine the first four ingredients in a large punch bowl. Strain maraschino cherry juice into the bowl, mix well, and add ice just before serving. Garnish individual servings with a cherry or float all of them on top of the punch in the bowl.

*Makes 40 servings.*

# Kitchen Sink Punch

Aptly named because it contains everything except the kitchen sink.

**1 10-ounce package frozen sliced strawberries in syrup**
**1 12-ounce can frozen orange juice concentrate**
**1 12-ounce can frozen lemonade concentrate**
**8 cups water**
**2 cups brewed black tea**
**2 cups white sugar**
**3½ cups light rum**
**3 trays frozen orange juice cubes**
**2 2-liter bottles lemon-lime soda, chilled**

Combine strawberries, orange juice concentrate, lemonade concentrate, water, and tea in a large punch bowl. Add sugar and rum and stir until sugar dissolves. Add orange juice cubes and soda immediately before serving.

*Makes 34 servings.*

# Peach & Strawberry Sangria

**1 750-ml bottle dry white wine**
**1 3/4 cups Essenia (a sweet dessert wine)**
**1 1/4 cups strawberries, washed, hulled and sliced**
**1 1/4 cups peach liqueur**
**3 peaches, pitted and quartered**
**1 large orange, cut crosswise into six slices**
**1 lime, cut crosswise into six slices**

Combine the above ingredients, bruising the orange slices slightly by pressing against the side of the pitcher. Allow the sangria to stand at room temperature for two hours or chill for four hours before serving in tall, ice-filled glasses.

*Makes 8 servings.*

# Roots & Wings: Georgia Sangria

With roots strongly anchored in the Mediterranean, traditional sangria has taken wing and headed to Georgia where peaches create a new sangria tradition.

**1 750-ml bottle white zinfandel**
**1/3 cup sugar**
**3/4 cup peach-flavored brandy**
**1 1/4 cups peach nectar**
**6 tablespoons thawed lemonade concentrate**
**4 peaches, peeled, pitted, and sliced**

Combine wine, sugar, brandy, nectar, and lemonade concentrate; mix until well blended. Add the sliced peaches and refrigerate overnight. Serve the next day from a large, ice-filled pitcher.

*Makes 6 to 8 servings.*

**Academic graduates, 1895.**
*(Courtesy Spelman College Archives)*

# Watermelon Daiquiri

Summer's signature fruit is blended to perfection in this refreshing offering. Cool and sweet, it's simply delicious!

**4 1/4 cups 3/4-inch seedless watermelon cubes**
**1/2 cup light rum**
**1 tablespoon Cointreau**
**1/4 cup powdered sugar**
**2 1/2 tablespoons fresh lime juice**
**3 tablespoons sour watermelon liqueur (such as Puckers, sold at most liqueur and grocery stores)**
**1/2 cup fresh strawberries, sliced**
**Fresh mint**

Seal the watermelon in a zip-top plastic freezer bag and freeze for 8 hours to form frozen melon cubes. Process the frozen watermelon and remaining ingredients (except mint) in a blender or food processor until smooth, stopping to scrape down the sides often. Pour into martini glasses, garnish with fresh mint, and serve immediately.

*Makes 4 servings.*

## Strawberries & Cream

A snappy pairing of ruby-red strawberries and velvety smooth cream.

**1 ounce strawberry schnapps**
**1 1/2 tablespoons sugar**
**2 ounces half and half**
**2 cups crushed ice**
**4 whole strawberries**
**Fresh strawberries to garnish**

Blend ingredients except strawberries with 2 cups crushed ice at high speed. Add strawberries and blend for 10 seconds. Serve in a parfait glass with a straw and garnish with a fresh strawberry.

*Makes 1 serving.*

## Peaches & Cream

A piña colada with a distinctive Southern accent.

**4 fresh peaches, pitted, peeled and quartered**
**1 cup chilled peach nectar**
**1/2 to 1 cup cream of coconut, chilled**
**3 ounces light rum**
**15 ice cubes**

Select one quartered peach and set aside. Place remaining three quartered peaches in a blender or food processor, blend until smooth. Add remaining ingredients except peach slices and blend until slushy. Pour into glasses and decorate rim with peach slice. Serve immediately.

*Makes 2 large drinks.*

*Note:* Cream of coconut can be found in most liquor stores or in some grocery gourmet sections.

Giles Hall faculty, ca. 1895.
*(Courtesy Spelman College Archives)*

# Amaretto Ice Cream Cappuccino

It wouldn't be morning in the South without a steaming hot cup of coffee. Now, enjoy an invigorating cup of coffee on even the hottest Southern day with this rich and frosty drink. Delicious any time of year.

**2 cups strong brewed Amaretto coffee, chilled**
**2/3 cup chocolate syrup, chilled**
**1/2 cup Amaretto liqueur**
**3 to 4 cups vanilla ice cream**
**Whipped cream**
**Cinnamon**

Combine coffee, chocolate syrup, and Amaretto. Combine with ice cream in a blender and blend smooth. Pour mixture into four tall, chilled glasses and garnish with whipped cream and cinnamon before serving.

*Makes 4 servings.*

Open house in Laura Spelman Hall, 1965.
*(Courtesy Spelman College Archives)*

*"If there is any nobler achievement in the annals of American womanhood than the founding of Spelman College . . . We confess that we know not of it."*
—*Opportunity,* May 1931

# Morris Brown College

*Knowledge is like a garden: If it is not cultivated, it cannot be harvested.*
—African proverb

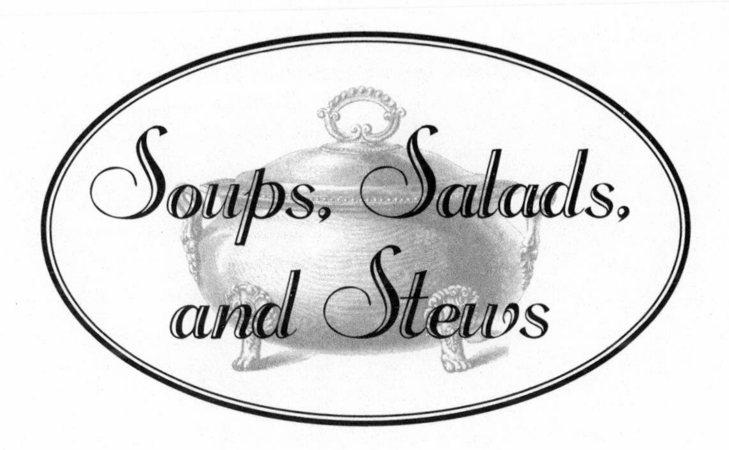

## A Church and College Built upon Principles of Independence and Self-Reliance

FOUNDED IN 1881 "for the Christian education of Negro boys and girls in Atlanta," Morris Brown College was named to honor the memory of the second consecrated bishop of the African Methodist Episcopal (AME) Church. The AME Church is Methodist in its basic doctrine and order of worship but broke away from the Methodist Church under Richard Allen, born a slave in 1760, because black Methodists could not receive communion until after all white members had been served.

On April 12, 1787, with the assistance of Absalom Jones, William White, and Dorus Ginnings, Richard Allen organized the Free African Society (FAS) in Philadelphia. This independent black organization was the first of its kind in America to dedicate itself to abolishing slavery and fostering self-help and self-dependence among people of color. From this Society came two groups: the Episcopalians and the Methodists. The leader of the Methodist group was Richard Allen, who wanted to be rid of the humiliation of segregated worship. The AME church is unique among religious denominations in the Western world in that its founding originated from sociological rather than theological differences. Fervently committed to the education of blacks, the church founded several AME schools, beginning in 1856 with Wilberforce University, the first private black college in America.

**Richard Allen**
*(Private collection)*

Following the Civil War, the congregation of Old Bethel, founded by slaves in 1840 and the oldest predominately African-American congregation in Atlanta, affiliated with the AME Church and would eventually become known as Big Bethel Church. In 1881, during the North

**Reverend Wesley J. Gaines and his wife, Mrs. Julia A. Gaines.**
*(Private collection of Mr. Herman Mason)*

Georgia Annual Conference at Big Bethel, the Reverend Wesley John Gaines introduced a resolution calling for the establishment in Atlanta of an institution for the "moral, spiritual, and intellectual growth of Negro boys and girls." In May 1885 the state of Georgia granted a charter to Morris Brown College of the AME Church. It is only fitting that Morris Brown College, the only college in Georgia started exclusively by African Americans, was a child of the AME church, a denomination started exclusively through the efforts of African Americans who refused to be segregated and treated as second-class citizens in their worship of a just God. The church wanted more education for their children than they had received, and felt it their duty to sacrifice in providing for it.

On October 15, 1885, 107 students and nine teachers walked into a crude wooden structure at the corner of Boulevard and Houston Streets in Atlanta. This occasion, which occurred just twenty years after the ratification of the 13th Amendment to the U.S. Constitution, marked the formal opening of the first educational institution in Georgia founded for and by African Americans. The school operated on the primary, secondary, and normal school levels until 1894, with a regular academic program and courses in tailoring, dressmaking, home economics, nursing education, commerce, and printing. A theological department for the training of ministers was established in 1894. The College Department began, graduating its first students four years later. The college changed its status to university in 1913, and as a result it was granted the right to establish and operate branch institutions of learning. The heavy financial burden imposed by the branches, however, made it necessary to discontinue them in 1929. And the present name, Morris Brown College, was restored. In 1932 Morris Brown College became the fourth member of the Atlanta University Center.

**The Early Years, ca. 1900.**
*(Private collection of Mr. Herman Mason)*

From its earliest days Morris Brown College sought to meet the educational needs of students from low socioeconomic backgrounds. The college, at that time, was largely dependent on a denomination whose constituency was primarily unskilled, untrained, and economically unstable. In order to survive, the college had to enroll a large segment of underachieving students whose parents were loyal supporters of the church that kept its doors open. What began as survival strategy for Morris Brown in 1881 became the liberation cry for black masses and the country at large in the 1960s. While Morris Brown has moved and grown since that time, its basic mission is still to serve as a place that welcomes all students, including those who might not be admitted into other schools for academic or economic reasons.

SOUPS, SALADS AND STEWS provided an efficient and inexpensive means of serving students highly nutritious meals. Many of the recipes that follow are for perennial Southern favorites, such as Navy Bean Soup, Garden Fresh Pea Soup, Vidalia Onion & Cucumber Salad, and Down Home Chicken Stew. Other offerings such as Caribbean Pumpkin and Black Bean Soup recognize the diversity of the student body and leadership. For instance, Professor William H. Crogman, born in the West Indies in 1841, later orphaned and befriended by a sea captain who recognized his intellectual gift, graduated with the first class of Atlanta University in 1876. Upon graduation, he accepted a faculty position and later served as its president. Read more about him on pages 256–58.

# *Soups*

**Soup is a wonderfully versatile dish. Served hot or cold, it can take you from early spring to late winter. Hearty or light, it's equally filling. From the deliciously cool chilled soups of spring and summer to the more substantial soups of winter, there are so many great recipes that you will never tire of it.**

## Southern Peanut Soup

1/3 cup coarsely chopped celery
1/3 cup coarsely chopped carrot
1/4 cup chopped onion
3/4 cup chicken broth
1 chicken bouillon cube
2 cups water, divided

1/2 cup creamy peanut butter
1/4 teaspoon black pepper
1/8 teaspoon cayenne pepper
Pinch nutmeg
1 tablespoon cornstarch
1/2 cup half and half
Chopped peanuts
Sliced scallions

Combine the first four ingredients in a saucepan and bring to a boil over medium-high heat. Reduce heat, cover and cook over low heat until the vegetables are soft and the onion is translucent, approximately 3 to 5 minutes. Add the bouillon cube and 1 1/2 cups water; cook uncovered until the bouillon cube dissolves. Remove saucepan from heat and allow to cool for 10 minutes before placing its contents into an electric blender or food processor and blending or pureeing it smooth. Return the pureed mixture to the saucepan; add peanut butter, black pepper, cayenne pepper, and nutmeg. Stir until

**The Boys of Summer—Morris Brown baseball team, ca. 1910.**
*(Private collection of Mr. Herman Mason)*

smooth and well blended. Combine the cornstarch and the remaining water and stir until it is well blended before stirring into the soup mixture. Bring to a rapid boil; reduce heat to low, and cook one minute. Stir in half and half. Cook over low heat uncovered, stirring constantly, until thoroughly heated. Garnish with chopped peanuts and scallions.

*Makes 4 servings.*

# West African Peanut Soup

This version of the traditional West African dish is puréed smooth rather than leaving the vegetables in chunks. It tastes wonderful and presents beautifully. Enjoy!

**2 tablespoons olive oil**
**2 cups chopped onion**

**Morris Brown College band—the beginnings of the Marching Wolverines.**
*(Private collection of Mr. Herman Mason)*

Morris Brown students, ca. 1921.
*(Private collection of Mr. Herman Mason)*

1 cup chopped yellow bell pepper
2 jalapeño peppers, seeded and chopped
3 large cloves of garlic, minced
1 teaspoon grated, peeled fresh ginger
1 cup chopped carrots
2 cups chopped sweet potatoes
4 cups beef stock
1 28-ounce can chopped tomatoes with juice
Up to 2 teaspoons of sugar
1 cup smooth peanut butter
Cayenne pepper to taste
Chopped green onions
Chopped roasted peanuts

Heat olive oil in a large stock pot over medium-high heat. Sauteé the onion, yellow pepper, jalapeño peppers, and garlic in the olive oil until it is translucent. Stir in ginger. Add carrots and sauté for an additional 2 to 3 minutes. Add sweet potatoes and stir in beef stock and tomatoes. Bring the mixture to a boil, reduce heat, and simmer 15 minutes or until the vegetables are fork

**At the Ready—Morris Brown gridiron warriors.**
*(Private collection of Mr. Herman Mason)*

tender. Allow mixture to cool sufficiently to handle without being burned. Add the vegetables and some of the cooking liquid to a blender or processor and purée in batches, if necessary. Return the purée to the cooking pot, stir in the sugar, and gently reheat as you add the peanut butter and stir until smooth. Add additional sugar to taste. I prefer less sugar and use only up to 1 tablespoon of sugar as opposed to the 1 tablespoon or more called for by some recipes. Add additional stock, water, or even tomato juice if a thinner soup is preferred. Garnish with plenty of chopped green onions and roasted peanuts.

*Makes 4 to 6 servings.*

# Cream of Pecan Soup

This delicious Southern favorite will soon be your favorite, too, no matter where you live.

**2 tablespoons unsalted butter**
**1/4 cup finely chopped onion**
**1 tablespoon all-purpose flour**
**2 cups chicken stock**
**1/2 teaspoon salt**

**1/8 teaspoon white pepper**
**1/8 teaspoon ground nutmeg**
**1 1/4 cups pecans**
**1 teaspoon minced celery leaves**
**1 3/4 cups half and half**
**4 small sprigs mint**

Melt butter in heavy medium saucepan over medium heat. When foam subsides, add onion and reduce the heat to low. Sauté the onion, stirring frequently, and continue to cook until the onion is soft but not browned, about 5 minutes. Stir in flour until thoroughly blended; cook, stirring, over low heat 1 minute. Gradually add the chicken stock while stirring constantly. Stir in the salt, pepper, and nutmeg. Next, add the pecans and celery leaves. Increase heat to medium and bring the soup to a rolling boil. Reduce heat to low and simmer the soup gently for 10 minutes, stirring occasionally. Stir in cream; simmer over very low heat 5 minutes to allow the cream to warm through. Adjust seasonings to taste. Ladle soup into individual warmed bowls. Garnish each bowl with a sprig of mint and serve at once.

*Makes 4 servings.*

**Morris Brown College girls basketball squad, 1935–36.**
*(Private collection of Mr. Herman Mason)*

**Morris Brown students, ca. 1940.**
*(Private collection of Mr. Herman Mason)*

# Georgia Peach Soup

A summertime sonata! It is the perfect prelude to a memorable meal. I have never seen a recipe to which I did not want to add a personal touch. This is an adaptation of a delicious recipe I found in *Coastal Magazine.*

**2 quarts chopped fresh peaches**
**1 cup dry white wine**
**1¼ cups peach schnapps**
**½ cup sugar**
**1¼ teaspoons chopped fresh mint**
**½ teaspoon ground cinnamon**
**⅛ teaspoon ground nutmeg**
**Pinch of allspice**
**2 cups half and half**
**½ cup heavy whipping cream**
**Mint leaves**
**Fresh raspberries**

Combine first 8 ingredients in a large saucepan and cook over medium heat for 15 minutes or until the peaches are fork tender and the liquid is reduced.

Remove from heat and allow the mixture to cool before processing it in a blender or food processor until smooth, stopping intermittently to scrape down the sides. Cover and chill. Just prior to serving, add the half and half and mix well. Return soup to the refrigerator, then whip cream until stiff peaks form. Ladle soup into individual serving bowls and garnish with a dollop of whipped cream, two or three mint leaves, and a raspberry.

*Makes 4 to 6 servings.*

# Old-Fashioned Potato Soup

Nothing says home more eloquently or makes coming home more pleasant than homemade soup.

**8 cups boiling chicken broth**
**1 teaspoon salt**
**8 cups raw potatoes, pared and chopped fine**

**Morris Brown students, ca. 1950.**
*(Private collection of Mr. Herman Mason)*

**1/4 cup chopped onion**
**1 leek, thinly sliced**
**1/2 cup butter**
**2 tablespoons flour**
**2 cups table cream**
**6 cups milk**
**2 tablespoons minced parsley**
**Parsley (optional)**

In a large pot, combine the broth and salt, and bring to a boil over medium-high heat. Add the potatoes, onion and leek. Reduce heat to medium and continue to cook until the mixture thickens, approximately 15 to 20 minutes. In a second large pot, melt butter over medium-high heat and stir in the flour until it is smooth. Add the cream and milk and cook until the mixture is thickened and smooth. Add the cream mixture to the potato mixture; add minced parsley and mix well. Serve piping hot with a garnish of additional chopped parsley.

*Makes 6 to 8 servings.*

# Garden Fresh Pea Soup

**1 pint water**
**1/8 teaspoon sugar**
**3 cups fresh peas (may substitute frozen)**
**1/2 cup chopped onion**
**3 tablespoons butter**
**3 tablespoons flour**
**1/2 teaspoon salt**
**1/8 teaspoon pepper**
**3 cups milk**
**1/2 teaspoon minced fresh mint**
**1/8 teaspoon nutmeg**

Combine water and sugar in a saucepan and bring to a rapid boil; add peas and onion, and cook over medium heat until the peas are soft but still bright green, 5 to 7 minutes. Allow peas to cool for 10 minutes before processing them smooth in a blender or food processor. Melt butter in the top of a double boiler, add flour, salt, and pepper; and then cook over medium-high heat until the butter mixture begins to bubble. Add milk and cook while continuously stirring over the hot mixture until it is smooth. Combine the pea mixture and cream sauce in the top of the double boiler. Stir in mint and nutmeg approximately 10 minutes before serving.

*Makes 6 servings.*

# Cream of Corn Soup

The pimento adds a festive touch to this delicious Southern favorite.

**3 strips bacon, finely chopped**
**1/4 cup finely chopped onion**
**2 1/4 cups fresh or frozen corn**
**3 tablespoons butter**
**3 tablespoons flour**
**2 cups milk**
**1 teaspoon salt**
**1/2 teaspoon pepper**
**1/3 cup chopped pimento**
**2 cups table cream**

Fry the bacon until crisp; add the onion and sauté until the onion is tender. Process the corn through a food processor or blender until finely chopped, but not pureed. Transfer to a saucepan, add corn to the bacon and onion mixture, and cook until the corn begins to brown. Reduce heat; add the butter and stir in the flour; cook slowly for 3 minutes. Add the milk, salt, and pepper and cook until thickened. Next, add the pimento and cream and heat and stir until smooth for 2 to 3 minutes.

*Makes 6 servings.*

# Chicken Velvet Soup

This soup and the one that follows call for cooked chicken. As a result, it provides a great opportunity to use leftover chicken or even turkey in a new and delicious way.

**1/3 cup butter**
**3/4 cup flour**
**6 cups hot chicken broth, divided**
**1 cup warm milk**
**1 1/4 cups warm table cream**
**1 3/4 cups finely diced cooked chicken breast**
**Salt and pepper to taste**

Melt butter over medium-high heat. Stir in flour and continue to stir and cook until the mixture is smooth and well blended. Add two cups of hot chicken broth and the warm milk and cream. Reduce heat and cook slowly, stirring frequently until the mixture thickens. Add remaining broth and chicken and increase heat to bring soup to a boil. Season to taste and enjoy!

*Makes 6 servings.*

# Chicken & Corn Soup

A quick and nutritious meal can be made from leftovers and some ingredients from your pantry. During the winter I try to keep on hand plenty of soup "fixins," such as broth, pasta noodles, tomato paste, etc., so when the soup opportunity presents itself, I am ready for the challenge.

**1 quart chicken broth**
**1/2 cup alphabet noodles**
**3/4 cup cooked chicken, finely diced**
**1/3 cup creamed corn**

**1 hard cooked egg, finely grated or mashed**
**1 teaspoon chopped parsley**

Heat chicken broth to boiling and add the noodles; bring to a second boil and cook an additional 3 minutes. Add chicken and corn; reduce heat to medium and cook an additional three minutes. Add remaining ingredients, cook an additional minute or two and serve with a few homemade croutons, if you are so inclined and have them on hand.

*Makes 4 servings.*

# Chicken & Rice Soup

I love this soup on a cold winter afternoon. It is truly comfort food. And its heady fragrance competes with its flavorful, warm broth to soothe you.

**1 3- to 3½-pound chicken, with neck and giblets (omit liver)**
**4 cloves of garlic, peeled and crushed**
**1 small onion, finely chopped**
**½ cup chopped green pepper**
**1 teaspoon salt**
**2 quarts chicken broth, divided**
**1½ cups long-grain rice**
**3 carrots, peeled, trimmed and sliced crosswise**
**3 stalks celery, trimmed and sliced crosswise**
**Pinch of saffron threads**

Place chicken, garlic, onion, green pepper, salt and 8 cups of the chicken broth into a large, heavy-bottomed pot and bring to a boil over high heat. Reduce heat to medium-low, cover, and simmer until the chicken is tender, approximately 1 hour. Use a slotted spoon to transfer the chicken to a plate and set aside to cool. Strain chicken broth into a large bowl, discard solids, and return broth to a clean pot. Add rice, carrots, celery, and saffron and bring to a boil over high heat. Reduce heat to medium and cook, uncovered, stirring occasionally until the rice is tender, approximately 15 minutes.

When the chicken is sufficiently cool to handle, remove the skin and bone and discard. Cut the meat into large chunks. Return the chicken to the pot with remaining broth. Season to taste with salt and pepper

*Makes 6 to 8 servings.*

# Chicken, Rice & Mushroom Soup

This light and easy-to-prepare version of chicken and rice soup can be appreciated anytime. However, its light flavor is especially enjoyable in early spring or fall.

**1/2 stick butter**
**1 1/4 cups mushrooms**
**1 1/4 cups sliced leeks**
**9 cups chicken broth**
**3 cups cooked chopped chicken**
**1 3/4 cups cooked rice**
**Salt and pepper to taste**

Melt butter in a large stockpot and sauté mushrooms and leeks over medium heat until tender. Add remaining ingredients; stir well, and simmer for 30 minutes.

*Makes 10 to 12 servings.*

# Chicken Vegetable Soup

As pleasing to the eye as it is to the palate!

**1 3- to 4-pound chicken, cut up into 8 or 9 pieces**
**3 quarts chicken broth**
**1 tablespoon salt**
**1/2 teaspoon garlic powder**
**1 teaspoon onion powder**
**1/3 cup chopped parsley**
**1/4 cup chopped dill**
**1 cup chopped celery**
**1 cup chopped carrots**
**1 cup fresh green beans cut into bite-size pieces**
**1/2 to 1 cup frozen corn kernels**
**5 new potatoes, quartered**
**3/4 cup finely chopped onions**
**2 tablespoons minced garlic**
**3 bay leaves**

Wash chicken thoroughly under cold running water and remove all visible fat. Place chicken and broth in a large stockpot and bring to a full boil over high heat. Skim off foam as it forms. Reduce heat to low and simmer an additional hour, skimming fat as it forms on the surface of the soup. Remove chicken and any skin or bones from the pot. Remove remaining skin and bone from the chicken pieces and discard. Chop chicken meat and add to the pot along with the remaining ingredients. Bring to a rolling boil, then reduce the heat to medium and continue to cook an additional 30 minutes or until the vegetables reach the desired degree of tenderness. For crisper vegetables reduce cooking time.

# Down-Home Chicken Stew

If it grows on the land, swims in the water, or is hunted or herded, you will find it in Southern soup or stew.

**2 3- to 3½-pound broiler fryers, washed under cold running water**
**3 quarts chicken broth**
**2 16-ounce cans chopped tomatoes, undrained**
**4½ cups whole kernel corn**
**2½ cups fresh butter beans**
**1 cup frozen cut okra**
**7 new potatoes, halved**
**2 large onions, chopped**
**1 tablespoon sugar**
**1 tablespoon salt**
**1 teaspoon pepper**
**½ cup butter**

Combine the chicken and broth in a large Dutch oven and bring to a boil. Cover, reduce heat, and simmer for 1 hour. Remove the chicken from the Dutch oven and allow the chicken to cool completely. Remove and discard the skin and bone from the chicken. Chop the chicken.

Combine 4 quarts of the reserved broth, chicken, and remaining ingredients in the Dutch oven; resume boiling. Reduce heat to low and simmer, uncovered, 4 to 5 hours, stirring often and adding additional broth or water as necessary to prevent scorching or burning

*Makes approximately 1 gallon.*

# Alphabet Beef Soup

This vegetable-laden alphabet soup says "back to school" so deliciously that your children will gladly heed its call. Start it when they leave for school and it will be ready when they come in from the cold.

**1 pound beef stew meat, cubed**
**8 cups beef broth**
**2 16-ounce packages frozen mixed vegetables**
**1/2 cup diced onion**
**2 14 1/2-ounce cans Italian-style diced tomatoes**
**2 8-ounce cans tomato sauce**
**1 beef bouillon cube (I use it instead of salt for added beef flavor)**
**1 cup alphabet noodles, uncooked**

Combine meat, beef broth, vegetables, onion, tomatoes, tomato sauce, and bouillon in a slow cooker; cover and cook on low 6 to 8 hours or until meat is tender. Turn control to high. Add noodles. Cover and cook on high 15 to 20 minutes or until noodles are cooked through. Serve hot.

*Makes 6 to 8 servings.*

# Beef, Barley & Mushroom Soup

This tasty blend of fresh vegetables and grains makes for an excellent "cold weather" meal when paired with your favorite green salad and fresh baked whole grain bread. It's early September and my mouth is watering at the thought of it!

**1 pound beef stew meat, cut in small pieces**
**3 14 1/2-ounce cans beef broth**
**2 cups thinly sliced carrots**
**2 ribs celery with tops, sliced**
**2 small onions, diced**
**1 1/2 cups fresh green beans cut into bite-size pieces**
**1 14 1/2-ounce can diced tomatoes**
**1 cup frozen lima beans**
**1 1/2 cups sliced mushrooms**
**2 teaspoons salt**
**2 cloves garlic, minced**
**2 bay leaves**

**1/4 cup fresh parsley, chopped**
**1/4 cup barley**

Place meat and beef broth into a large stockpot and bring to a rapid boil. Reduce heat and simmer for 2 hours. Add remaining ingredients except barley and cook an additional 30 to 40 minutes. Add additional broth as needed to allow ingredients to boil freely without sticking. Add barley and cook until barley is tender. Check package directions for approximate cooking time. Serve with green salad and crusty bread.

*Makes 6 to 8 servings.*

# Vegetable Beef Soup

This hearty beef stew–like soup will quickly become a favorite with your family and friends. Serve it up hot with a wedge of sour cream cornbread or one of the other delicious cornbreads featured in the Hot from the Oven section.

**3 tablespoons all-purpose flour**
**1 tablespoon paprika**
**2 teaspoons salt**
**1/2 teaspoon black pepper**
**1/4 teaspoon ground cumin**
**1 3- to 3 1/2-pound boneless beef chuck cut into 1-inch cubes**
**1/4 cup vegetable oil**
**2 medium onions, chopped**
**1 cup chopped green pepper**
**3 cloves garlic, peeled and finely chopped**
**1 28-ounce can stewed tomatoes, undrained**
**2 quarts beef broth, divided**
**1 bay leaf**
**2 tablespoons tomato paste**
**7 unpeeled new potatoes, halved**

**4 medium carrots, sliced**
**1 11-ounce can whole kernel corn, drained**
**1 cup French cut green beans**

In a large, zip top plastic bag, combine the flour, paprika, salt, black pepper, and cumin. Seal and shake to mix. Add the beef a few pieces at a time and shake to coat. In a large heavy-bottomed pot or soup kettle, heat the vegetable oil over medium-high heat. Brown the beef in small batches, on all sides, for approximately five minutes. Stir in the onions, green pepper, and garlic; stir and sauté for five minutes or until onion is softened. Add stewed tomatoes; four cups of the beef broth, scraping up any brown sediment stuck to the bottom of the pot; and bay leaf. Bring to a boil and reduce heat, partially cover and simmer for thirty minutes, stirring occasionally. Stir in the tomato paste. Reduce heat to medium, partially cover the pot, and simmer until meat is fork tender, approximately 30 minutes.

Add potatoes, carrots, corn, green beans, and remaining broth to the pot, reduce heat to medium-low, and continue to cook with the pot partially covered until the potatoes are soft, approximately 35 to 40 minutes. Add additional seasoning to taste.

*Makes 8 to 10 servings.*

# Navy Bean Soup

This soup is a tradition in my family. My dad could be counted on to prepare it at least once a week.

**1 pound dried navy beans**
**2 meaty ham hocks**
**2 tablespoons bacon drippings or vegetable oil**
**1 medium onion, peeled and finely diced**
**1 large clove garlic, finely minced**
**2 quarts chicken broth**
**Salt and freshly ground pepper**

Pick over beans and remove any stones or any other foreign objects. Rinse beans, place them in a large non-reactive container with sufficient water to cover by 2 inches, and soak overnight. Rinse ham hocks and place them in a large Dutch oven with chicken broth and sufficient water to cover. Bring ham hocks to a rapid boil, reduce heat to low, cover, and simmer for one hour. Meanwhile, heat drippings or vegetable oil in a medium skillet over medium heat; add the onions and garlic and cook, stirring frequently, until the onions are just beginning to brown, 3 to 5 minutes. Drain the beans and rinse again before adding them to the Dutch oven. Add onions and remaining ingredients to the pot; reduce heat, and simmer beans over low heat until they are tender, stirring occasionally. When beans are tender, remove ham hocks and allow them to cool before cutting the meat from the bones, chopping, and returning it to the pot. Discard skin, bone, and excess fat. Use a large cooking spoon to mash some of the beans against the side of the pot and stir to thicken the soup and make it creamier. Season this heart-warming soup to taste with salt and pepper and serve piping hot with a side of cornbread.

*Makes 8 to 10 servings.*

# Three-Bean Soup

A confetti of colorful beans and riotous color makes this soup as beautiful as it is delicious. Enjoy!

**2 cups dried navy beans**
**1 cup dried red beans**
**1½ cups dried black beans**
**2 ham hocks**
**3 10½-ounce cans chicken broth**
**3⅔ cups water**
**2 large onions, finely chopped**
**1 cup sliced carrots**
**1 cup sliced celery**

**2 large cloves garlic, finely minced**
**1 tablespoon minced parsley**
**1 teaspoon salt**
**1 teaspoon finely minced fresh basil**
**1 teaspoon dried oregano**
**3 cups chopped turnip greens**

Pick over beans and remove any stones or other foreign objects. Rinse beans, place them in a large non-reactive container with sufficient water to cover by 2 inches, and soak overnight. Rinse ham hocks and place them in a large Dutch oven with chicken broth and sufficient water to cover. Bring ham hocks to a rapid boil, reduce heat to low, cover, and simmer for one hour. Drain the beans and rinse again before adding them to the Dutch oven. Add onions and next 7 ingredients to the pot; reduce temperature and simmer beans over low heat until they are tender, stirring occasionally. When beans are tender, remove ham hocks; cut meat from the bones, chop, and return it to the pot. Add greens during the last 30 minutes of cooking time, stirring occasionally.

*Makes 8 to 10 servings.*

# Red Bean Soup with Smoked Turkey

This delicious soup is a great source of protein. The addition of the chunks of turkey makes it a one-pot meal that your family will really enjoy. With a more demanding writing and speaking schedule I have rediscovered the many benefits of one-pot and crock-pot cooking.

**1 pound dried red beans**
**3/4 cup chopped onions**
**1/2 cup chopped green peppers**
**3 cloves garlic, minced**
**2 quarts unsalted chicken broth**

**2 1/2 cups smoked turkey, cut in 1-inch cubes**
**Salt and pepper to taste**
**4 cups cooked rice**

Place all ingredients except rice and seasonings, in crock-pot; cover and cook 6 hours on the "High" setting or overnight on the "Low" setting. Check pot often and add additional broth as necessary to prevent sticking. When beans are finished add salt and pepper to taste. Just prior to serving, stir in the rice and adjust seasoning to taste.

*Makes 8 servings.*

# Jamaican Red Pea Soup

Some of the best Jamaican food, outside of the islands, must be in Atlanta. Usually my first stop after arriving in the city is one of the plethora of Jamaican restaurants located there. I am particularly fond of those near the AUC. However, timing is everything, so arrive slightly ahead of the lunch and dinner hour rush. I love the flavor and intensity of this soup. The Scotch bonnet pepper called for in the recipe is extremely hot. Extreme diners, enjoy! All others beware.

**2 cups dried kidney beans, soaked and drained**
**10 cups water**
**2 tablespoons vegetable oil**
**2 medium onions, diced**
**1 large green pepper, diced**
**4 cloves garlic, minced**
**1 Scotch bonnet pepper, seeded and minced**
**6 green onions**
**1 large carrot, diced**
**1 sweet potato, peeled and cubed**
**2 teaspoons thyme**

**1 cup coconut milk**
**1/2 teaspoon allspice**
**1/2 teaspoon black pepper**
**1 teaspoon salt**

Pick over beans to remove foreign objects and soak overnight in sufficient cold water to cover beans by 2 inches. Drain and rinse beans before cooking. Place in a large soup pot and add water. Bring beans to a quick boil and reduce heat to medium. Cook for 1 hour, adding additional water as necessary to prevent the beans from sticking. Drain beans, reserving 5 cups of the liquid, and set aside. Sauté the onions, green pepper, and garlic in the oil for 5 to 7 minutes. Return beans to the pot containing the sautéed vegetables. Add cooking liquid and remaining ingredients except salt. Simmer for 1 to 1 1/2 hours over low heat. Add salt to taste.

*Makes 8 servings.*

# Jamaican Pepper Pot Soup

There are as many versions of Jamaican pepper pot soup as there are cooks. This one, made simply with shrimp, is one of my favorites.

**1 1/4 cups green bell pepper, seeded and chopped**
**3/4 cup minced onion**
**3 tablespoons vegetable oil**
**3 cloves garlic, minced**
**1 teaspoon salt**
**1/2 teaspoon thyme leaves, crushed**
**1/2 teaspoon marjoram, crushed**
**1/2 teaspoon rosemary, crushed**
**1 ripe Scotch bonnet pepper, whole**
**6 cups chicken stock**
**1 10-ounce package frozen okra, sliced**

**1 cup chopped fresh spinach**
**2 pounds (50 to 60) small shrimp, peeled and deveined**
**1 cup canned cream of coconut**
**10 lime slices**

Combine green pepper, minced onion, oil, and minced garlic in a large stockpot; sauté over medium heat until the onions are limp and transparent. Add salt, thyme, marjoram, rosemary, pepper, and chicken stock and heat to boiling. Reduce heat; simmer, covered, 30 minutes. Add okra and spinach and cook an additional 30 to 40 minutes. Add shrimp and coconut milk. Simmer until shrimp are cooked, about 5 minutes. Ladle into individual serving dishes and garnish with lime slices.

Note: The Scotch bonnet pepper is extremely hot. Take care that it does not burst during cooking, and remove it from the pot immediately after the soup is done.

*Makes 10 servings.*

## Chicken Pepper Pot Soup

For the chicken lover in you!

**1 3- to 3½-pound chicken, cut into 8 pieces**
**10 cups chicken broth**
**8 whole cloves**
**2 bay leaves**
**3 thin slices peeled fresh ginger**
**2 tablespoons turmeric**
**½ teaspoon cayenne pepper, to taste**
**1 tablespoon curry powder**
**½ teaspoon black pepper**
**1 15-ounce can chickpeas, rinsed**
**4 tablespoons unsalted butter**
**3 cloves of garlic, minced**
**4 tablespoons all-purpose flour**

**1 cup canned coconut milk**
**½ cup heavy cream**
**Lemon wedges**
**Fresh cilantro**
**Hot cooked white rice**

In a large enamel or stainless steel soup pot combine chicken and broth, bring to a rapid boil, reduce heat, and simmer, partly covered, for approximately 1 hour or until the chicken is tender and falls from the bones. While the chicken is simmering, add the cloves, bay leaf, ginger, turmeric, cayenne, curry powder, and black pepper. Skim away foam as it rises to the surface, then re-cover partly and continue to simmer. When the chicken is done, remove it and discard skin and bones. Pull chicken meat into bite-size pieces and set aside. Skim and strain soup and return to rinsed pot.

Purée chickpeas in blender or food processor with 1 to 2 cups of soup as needed. Pour puréed chickpeas with their liquid back into soup and return to a simmer with the pot partially covered.

Recipe can be prepared up to this point and stored, covered, in the refrigerator for 1 day.

About 30 minutes before serving, add chicken pieces to soup and bring to a simmer; add additional broth if the soup becomes too thick. Melt butter in a small skillet and when hot, sauté garlic for 3 to 4 minutes or until it just begins to brown. Sprinkle flour over the mixture, stirring and sautéing for about 5 minutes until it turns bright yellow. Beat into simmering soup with a whisk and cook 10 minutes.

Stir in coconut milk and cream and simmer gently for approximately 5 minutes. Adjust seasonings to taste, and then simmer for 5 minutes.

Serve in small bowls or cups garnished with lemon wedges and cilantro. If serving as a main course, mound portions of rice on side plates.

*Makes 4 to 6 servings.*

# Caribbean Pumpkin & Black Bean Soup

High in fiber, this hearty and flavorful soup is perfect for fall!

**2 teaspoons ground cumin**
**2 15-ounce cans white pumpkin purée**
**2 15-ounce cans black beans, drained**
**2 14-ounce cans light unsweetened coconut milk**
**2 cups canned vegetable broth**
**8 tablespoons chopped fresh cilantro, divided**
**4 teaspoons fresh lime juice**
**1½ teaspoons grated lime peel**
**Salt or salt substitute to taste**
**Pepper**

Stir cumin in heavy medium saucepan over medium heat 30 seconds to release the flavor. Add pumpkin, beans, coconut milk, broth, and 5 tablespoons of the cilantro. Bring soup to a boil, stirring constantly. Reduce heat to medium-low and simmer 3 minutes to blend flavors. Mix in lime juice and lime peel. Season the soup to taste with salt (or salt substitute) and pepper. Ladle soup into bowls. Sprinkle with remaining 3 tablespoons of the cilantro.

*Makes 4 servings.*

# Jamaican Cream of Pumpkin Soup

**2 tablespoons butter**
**2 large onions, finely chopped**
**2¼ pounds pumpkin, peeled and cut in chunks**
**4 cups chicken stock**
**Salt and black pepper to taste**
**1 cup light cream**

**Dash of Tabasco**
**Finely minced parsley**
**Roasted shelled pumpkin seeds**

Heat the butter in a saucepan and sauté the onion until transparent. Add pumpkin and chicken stock and simmer, covered, until the pumpkin is tender. Cool slightly and put through a sieve or process for a few seconds in an electric blender. Return the soup to the saucepan and season it with salt and pepper. Add the cream and Tabasco and gently reheat. Garnish with parsley and roasted pumpkin seeds.

*Makes 6 servings.*

# Salads

**Salads—cool, crunchy, and delicious—are often the perfect accompaniment to soup. And as with soup there is an endless variety from which to select. We'll start with a marinated Vidalia onion and sliced tomato salad and end with an adaptation of an African salad. While our adaptation is slightly saucier than the peach salad, it's not impertinent.**

## Marinated Vidalia Onion & Sliced Tomato Salad

Ummm ummm good. One taste and I am seated at my grandmother's table again, saying grace and asking my cousin to pass the salad.

**2 medium Vidalia onions, sliced thin**
**1 cup warm water**
**1/2 cup sugar**
**1/4 cup white vinegar**
**1/4 cup mayonnaise**
**1/8 teaspoon celery seeds**
**1/8 teaspoon cayenne pepper**
**1 large tomato, sliced thin**
**Mayonnaise**
**Paprika**
**Bread and butter pickles**

Separate onion slices into rings. Combine water, sugar, and vinegar, stir until sugar dissolves. Pour mixture over onion rings and refrigerate to marinate for 3 to 4 hours or overnight. Drain and reserve marinade from onion rings.

Arrange onion rings in a shallow serving dish with tomatoes. Stir mayonnaise and celery seeds into 3/4 cup of the reserved marinade and pour over salad. Garnish with a small dollop of mayonnaise, paprika, and a scattering of bread and butter pickles before serving.

*Makes 6 servings.*

# Vidalia Onion & Cucumber Salad

**3 cups peeled, seeded, and thinly sliced cucumbers**
**1 1/2 cups thinly sliced Vidalia onions or 2 small onions**
**2/3 cup grated carrot**
**1/2 cup white vinegar**
**1/4 cup sugar**
**2 1/2 tablespoons fresh dill, chopped fine**
**1/2 teaspoon salt**
**1/4 teaspoon ground black pepper**
**6 1/4-inch slices of vine ripened tomatoes**
**6 boiled egg wedges**

In a medium-sized bowl combine the cucumbers, Vidalia onions, and carrot. Set aside. Prepare dressing by combining the next five ingredients, mix well, and pour over the vegetables. Toss to coat and refrigerate three to four hours or until ready to serve. Using a slotted spoon, place a heaping mound of cucumber salad on a tomato slice and garnish with an egg wedge. The cucumber salad is also excellent when served alone.

*Makes 6 servings.*

# Old-Fashioned Cucumber Salad

I love cucumbers and this recipe is among my many favorites.

**2 medium unpeeled cucumbers, scored and very thinly sliced**
**1 small white onion, very thinly sliced**
**1/4 cup white vinegar**
**2 tablespoons chopped onion**
**1 tablespoon lemon juice**
**1 teaspoon celery seeds**
**1/4 teaspoon minced dill**
**3/4 teaspoon salt**
**1/8 teaspoon pepper**

Arrange cucumber and onion in a shallow serving dish. In a separate bowl, combine the remaining ingredients, mix well, pour over cucumbers, cover, and chill 4 to 6 hours before serving.

*Makes 6 servings.*

# Cucumber & Onion Salad

This is a great side salad spring, summer, winter, or fall! It complements almost everything without being overpowering.

**1 large cucumber**
**1 medium red onion**
**1 large tomato**
**1/4 cup finely chopped parsley**
**1/4 cup fresh squeezed lime juice**
**1/4 cup olive oil**
**Salt and pepper**

Cut up cucumbers, onion, and tomato into small cubes. Place in a salad bowl, add parsley, and lightly toss together. Combine remaining ingredients and use to dress the salad. Salt and pepper the salad to taste; and refrigerate to chill.

*Makes 4 to 6 servings.*

## Marinated Garden-Fresh Tomatoes

Nothing is as delicious as garden-fresh tomatoes. The fresh parsley and basil only enhance their appeal. Don't refrigerate your tomatoes. Once refrigerated, tomatoes stop ripening and lose their taste. Keep this in mind when bringing tomatoes home that are underripe when they are shipped in order to reach their destination in an unspoiled condition.

**4 large tomatoes**
**1 1/2 tablespoons chopped fresh parsley**
**1 1/2 tablespoons chopped fresh basil**
**1/3 cup vegetable oil**
**1/4 cup red wine vinegar**
**1 teaspoon salt**
**1/2 teaspoon sugar**
**1/4 teaspoon coarsely ground black pepper**
**1 clove garlic, finely minced**

Slice tomatoes 1/2-inch thick and arrange in a shallow dish. Set aside. Garnish tomatoes with parsley and basil. Combine the remaining ingredients, mix well and pour over the tomato slices. Cover and marinate in the refrigerator for several hours or overnight.

*Makes 6 servings.*

# Sweet Pepper & Onion Salad

1 medium green pepper, thinly sliced
1 medium yellow pepper, thinly sliced
1 medium red pepper, thinly sliced
1 red onion, sliced thin and separated into rings
1 clove garlic, minced
1/2 cup cider vinegar
1/2 cup water
4 1/2 teaspoons vegetable oil
2 tablespoons minced fresh basil
2 1/4 tablespoons sugar
1/4 teaspoon salt
1/8 teaspoon black pepper

Arrange the pepper and onion slices in a shallow serving dish. In a separate, small mixing bowl, combine the garlic, vinegar, water, and vegetable oil, mix well and pour over the salad. Refrigerate overnight. Just before serving, add the basil, sugar, salt, and pepper and mix well.

*Makes 6 servings.*

# Marinated Corn Salad

The variety of color and flavor make this a particularly inviting summer salad. This old school favorite receives an A+ for its eye and taste appeal.

2 cups yellow corn cut from the cob (approximately 4 to 5 ears)
1/3 cup water
1/3 cup chopped red pepper
1/4 cup chopped onion
1/2 cup chopped celery
3 tablespoons thinly sliced green onion
1 tablespoon chopped fresh parsley
1/4 cup vegetable oil

**1 tablespoon cider vinegar**
**1/2 teaspoon sugar**
**1/2 teaspoon salt**
**1/2 teaspoon dry mustard**
**1/4 teaspoon pepper**

Combine corn and water in a medium-sized saucepan. Bring to a boil over medium-high heat and simmer 8 to 9 minutes or until the corn is crisp-tender. Drain, combine the corn with the pepper and the next four ingredients. Set aside. Combine the remaining ingredients and mix well. Dress salad, cover, and marinate for 4 hours or overnight before serving.

*Makes 6 servings.*

# Zesty Black-Eyed Pea Salad

Saucy but not impertinent, its zesty flavor demands notice. So do include it in a salad and bread supper. It pairs well with the Marinated Corn and Tomato and the Vidalia Onion salads.

**2 16-ounce cans black-eyed peas**
**1/2 cup chopped celery**
**1/3 cup finely chopped Bermuda onion**
**1 green pepper, stemmed, seeded, and chopped**
**1 large tomato, peeled, seeded, and chopped**
**1 jalapeño pepper, stemmed, seeded, and chopped**
**3 cloves garlic, minced**
**3 green onions, sliced, include the tops**
**1 8-ounce bottle zesty Italian salad dressing**

Combine the above ingredients in a large non-reactive bowl and toss together to blend. Cover and chill 8 hours, stirring occasionally. Drain and serve well chilled. Save marinade and add it and another can of beans to any remaining salad. Your family is sure to want more!

*Makes 8 servings.*

# Honeyed Harvest Carrot Salad

Even your children will enjoy eating vitamin A–rich carrots prepared in this manner.

**1 pound shredded carrots**
**1 8-ounce can crushed pineapple, drained**
**3/4 cup miniature marshmallows**
**1/2 cup flaked coconut**
**1/2 cup raisins**
**3 tablespoons sour cream**
**3 tablespoons lemon juice**
**3 tablespoons honey**
**Chopped toasted pecans**

Combine first 5 ingredients in a large mixing bowl and set aside. Combine the remaining ingredients except the toasted pecans, pour over the carrot salad, and mix well. Cover and refrigerate 8 hours or overnight. Garnish with toasted pecans immediately before serving.

*Makes 6 servings*

# Turnip Slaw

Turnips elevate this delicious Southern favorite to new heights. Fresh turnips should have a smooth, firm appearance and feel heavy for their size.

**3 cups shredded turnips**
**1 3/4 cups shredded carrot**
**3/4 cup raisins**
**2 tablespoons sour cream**
**3/4 cup mayonnaise**
**1 tablespoon lemon juice**
**1 tablespoon sugar**

Combine the above ingredients in a large bowl. Mix the salad well, and refrigerate to chill before serving.

*Makes 6 to 8 servings.*

## Festive Apple Slaw

Apples are a tasty and healthy addition to this slaw.

**1/4 cup sour cream**
**1/2 cup mayonnaise**
**1/4 teaspoon celery seeds**
**1 1/4 teaspoons sugar**
**1 teaspoon white vinegar**
**Pinch of salt**
**1 1/2 cups grated cabbage**
**1 1/4 cups grated red cabbage**
**1/2 cup grated carrots**
**1 unpeeled apple, cored and coarsely chopped**

Combine the first six ingredients and mix well to make the salad dressing. In a large bowl, combine the dressing and remaining ingredients and refrigerate before serving.

*Makes 6 to 8 servings.*

## Waldorf Salad, Georgia Style

The peach preserves offer the perfect twist to this classical favorite!

**5 medium Red Delicious apples, unpeeled**
**Juice of 1 lemon**
**1/2 cup sliced celery**

**1/2 cup chopped pecans**
**1/2 cup raisins**
**1/3 to 1/2 cup mayonnaise**
**1/4 cup peach preserves**
**Lettuce leaves**

Wash apples and pat dry before coring and cutting them into 1/2-inch cubes. Sprinkle with lemon juice to prevent discoloration. Combine apples with celery, pecans, and raisins. In a separate bowl combine mayonnaise and peach preserves. Mix well and add just enough to salad mixture to reach the desired consistency. Salad should be firm and chunky, not soupy. Serve apple salad on lettuce leaves.

*Makes 6 servings.*

# Georgia Peach Salad with Raspberry Vinaigrette Dressing

This luscious peach salad is perfectly at home on a formal dinner table or at a private alfresco dinner for two beneath Georgia's star-strewn sky.

**4 peaches, sliced**
**Mixed greens**
**3/4 cup coarsely chopped pecans, toasted**
**1/3 cup raspberry preserves**
**2 1/4 tablespoons red wine vinegar**
**1 tablespoon vegetable oil**

Arrange peaches on serving plate over a bed of mixed greens. Sprinkle with pecans. Combine remaining ingredients and mix well. Drizzle over fruit.

*Makes 4 to 6 servings.*

# Chicken Pecan Fan Salad with Peach Vinaigrette

The hand that the lady fans with may be otherwise occupied if this tasty salad is served at your next summer luncheon or garden party. Enjoy!

**4 1/4 cooked chicken, cubed**
**1 3/4 cups toasted pecans, chopped**
**1/3 cup sliced green onions**
**1/3 cup raisins**
**1/2 cup mayonnaise**
**1/4 cup Peach Vinaigrette (recipe follows)**
**3 peach wedges, peeled**
**Salad greens**

Combine the first four ingredients in a large bowl and mix gently to combine. In a separate bowl, combine the mayonnaise and peach vinaigrette and pour it over the chicken mixture and toss gently. Refrigerate for at least 2 hours before serving. Arrange beds of lettuce leaves on individual salad plates. Arrange a "fan" of three wedges of sliced peaches on the salad greens with half of it extending onto the plate. Spoon approximately 3/4 cup of salad on each bed, taking care not to completely cover the fan. Drizzle an additional teaspoon of vinaigrette over the salad before serving.

*Makes 6 servings.*

## PEACH VINAIGRETTE

**1 cup peach preserves**
**1/4 cup peach nectar**
**1/4 cup white vinegar**
**1 teaspoon seasoning salt**
**1 teaspoon Italian seasoning**

Combine all of the above ingredients in a blender or food processor and puree until well blended. Refrigerate until ready to use.

*Makes 1 1/2 cups.*

# Chicken, Pineapple & Peppered Pecan Salad

I love the crunchy texture and subtle interplay of flavors in this salad, which is perfect luncheon fare.

**1 teaspoon salt**
**1/2 tablespoon coarsely ground black pepper**
**1/8 teaspoon onion powder**
**1/4 cup sugar**
**1 cup pecan pieces**
**4 cups cubed, cooked chicken**
**1 cup cubed pineapple pieces, well drained**
**1/2 cup mayonnaise**
**1/4 cup sour cream**
**1/2 cup sliced green onions, include tops**
**Salt**
**White or black pepper, to taste**
**Lettuce leaves**

Lightly oil a cookie sheet and set aside. Combine salt, pepper, onion powder, and sugar and stir to blend. Heat heavy cast-iron skillet and add pecans. Place pan over high heat and stir pecans for 1 minute while pan is heating. Sprinkle half the sugar mix on pecans and continue to stir for 1 minute. While cooking, add remaining sugar mixture and continue to stir until sugar mixture is completely melted. Remove nuts and immediately place on pre-oiled cookie sheet. Set pecans aside and allow them to cool completely. Combine chicken, pineapple, mayonnaise, sour cream, and green onions in a large bowl; mix to combine and add salt and pepper to taste. Add pecans and toss well to coat and serve immediately. If desired, serve salad on a bed of lettuce leaves.

*Makes 6 to 8 servings.*

# Jamaican Jerk Chicken Salad

If you like a little drama, you will love this spicy salad drama queen.

**1 head Belgian endive lettuce**
**2 15-ounce cans black beans, rinsed and drained**
**1/3 cup each red, yellow, and orange pepper, chopped**
**1/2 cup ripe papaya, peeled and diced**
**1/3 cup chopped red onions**
**1/3 cup sliced celery**
**Dressing (recipe follows)**
**2 cups coarsely chopped Jerk Chicken Breast (recipe follows)**
**1 ripe mango, peeled, seeded, and sliced**
**1 ripe avocado, sliced into 8 wedges**

Wash lettuce and set aside to drain. Arrange a bed of lettuce on each of four plates. In a medium bowl combine the remaining ingredients except chicken, sliced mango, and avocado. Prepare dressing (see recipe below), pour 1/3 cup of it over the black beans, and toss lightly. Divide the salad among the four plates by spooning it on top of the lettuce. Top each individual salad with 1/2 cup of the chopped chicken. Garnish the side of each plate with the mango slices and two avocado wedges.

## DRESSING

**1/2 teaspoon salt**
**1/4 teaspoon ground cumin**
**1/4 teaspoon allspice**
**1/8 teaspoon chili powder**
**Pinch ground nutmeg**
**Pinch ground cinnamon**
**1 clove garlic, minced**
**1/4 teaspoon fresh thyme**
**1 teaspoon fresh ginger, grated**
**1/4 cup vegetable oil**
**1 tablespoon + 2 teaspoons fresh lime juice**

**1 tablespoon honey**
**1/4 teaspoon ground red pepper**

Combine the beans, peppers, papaya and red onion in a salad bowl, and mix gently. Combine the remaining ingredients in a tightly covered jar, shake well, and pour over salad just before serving.

*Makes 4 to 6 servings.*

## JERK CHICKEN BREAST

**1 tablespoon ground allspice**
**1 tablespoon dried thyme**
**1 3/4 teaspoons cayenne pepper**
**1 1/2 teaspoons freshly ground black pepper**
**1 1/2 teaspoons ground sage**
**1 teaspoon ground nutmeg**
**1 teaspoon ground cinnamon**
**2 tablespoons minced garlic**
**1 tablespoon sugar**
**1/4 cup olive oil**
**1/4 cup soy sauce**
**1/2 cup white vinegar**
**1/2 cup orange juice**
**1/4 cup lime juice**
**2 Scotch bonnet peppers (habañero), seeded and finely chopped**
**5 green onions, finely chopped**
**1 1/4 cups onion, finely chopped**
**2 tablespoons grated ginger**
**4 to 6 chicken breasts, washed and trimmed of fat**

In a large bowl, combine the first nine ingredients and mix to blend. Slowly add the olive oil, soy sauce, vinegar, orange juice and lime juice to the bowl while beating the mixture with a wire whisk. Add the peppers, onions and grated ginger to the bowl and mix well. Place chicken breasts in the marinade and turn once to coat. Marinate for at least 2 to 3 hours, longer if possible, turning once at the midway point.

Remove the breasts from the marinade and cook on a preheated grill for approximately 6 minutes on each side or until fully cooked. While the chicken is grilling use the leftover marinade to occasionally baste it. Chicken is done when the thickest part is pierced with a fork and the juices run clear.

# Bread & Butter Pickle Potato Salad

It's likely that this recipe will conjure up the old-fashioned taste of your grandmother's "forgotten" potato salad recipe. Grocery store relishes don't quite capture that delicious taste. Take a bite and remember summers in the South or in the country at grandma's house.

**4 pounds new potatoes, scrubbed**
**1 small yellow onion, finely chopped**
**1 cup finely chopped bread and butter pickles plus 1/2 cup of juice from the jar**
**1 cup mayonnaise**
**2 tablespoons cider vinegar**
**1 large red pepper, stemmed, seeded, and chopped**
**3/4 cup fresh parsley, minced**
**Salt and pepper to taste**

Bring potatoes to a rapid boil over high heat; reduce heat and simmer until the potatoes are fork tender, approximately 20 to 30 minutes. Drain well and allow to stand until sufficiently cool to handle.

In a large bowl combine the chopped onion, chopped pickles, pickle juice, mayonnaise, and vinegar. Once your potatoes are cool, cube them and add the red peppers. Pour the salad dressing over the salad and mix gently. Allow the salad to rest at room temperature for 15 minutes before adding 1/2 cup of the parsley. Add salt and pepper to taste, mix well to blend, and transfer salad to a serving bowl. Garnish with remaining parsley and serve.

*Makes 12 servings.*

# Bread & Butter Pickles

Bread and butter pickles, once only canned in home kitchens, are now available in stores. But if you have a hankering to make your own, here is the recipe:

**4 quarts sliced pickling cucumbers**
**8 medium white onions, sliced**
**1/3 cup pickling salt**
**4 cloves of garlic, halved**
**Cracked ice**
**4 cups + 2 tablespoons sugar**
**3 cups cider vinegar**
**2 tablespoons mustard seed**
**1/2 teaspoon crushed red pepper**
**1 1/2 teaspoons turmeric**
**1 1/2 teaspoons celery seed**
**18 whole allspice**

In a 6- to 8-quart stockpot combine cucumbers, onions, pickling salt, and garlic. Add two inches of cracked ice. Cover the pot and refrigerate pickle mixture for 3 hours. Drain and remove the garlic halves from the mixture.

Add the sugar, vinegar, mustard seed, crushed red pepper, turmeric, celery seed, and allspice to the cucumber mixture and bring to a boil. Pack the hot cucumber mixture with liquid into hot, sterilized (follow manufacturer's directions) canning jars, leaving 1/2 inch of headspace. Wipe rims, adjust lids, and process in boiling water for 10 minutes. Remove jars and cool on racks for 10 minutes.

*Makes 7 pints.*

# Jamaican Potato Salad

Yah, mon, it's a little different from its American cousin, which follows, but it's a delicious accompaniment to Jerk Chicken and a multitude of other Caribbean dishes.

**4¼ cups cooked potatoes, diced**
**3 large boiled eggs, diced**
**¼ cup sliced green onions**
**2 tablespoons butter, melted**
**1 clove garlic**
**½ teaspoon garlic powder**
**1 cup mayonnaise**
**¼ teaspoon black pepper**
**¼ cup chopped celery**
**¼ cup corn**
**¼ cup baby peas, blanched**
**¼ cup chopped carrots**
**¼ teaspoon salt**

Combine the above ingredients and mix well. Serve warm or cold.

*Makes 6 to 8 servings.*

# All-American Potato Salad

Enjoy this perennial favorite with any food—traditional soul food, barbecue, grilled meats, Southern traditional Sunday dinner favorites like turkey or ham. Are you hungry yet?

**1½ pounds baking potatoes, halved**
**¾ cup finely chopped red onion**
**¾ cup finely chopped green pepper**
**⅓ cup finely chopped celery**
**⅓ cup sweet pickle relish**

**8 large hard-boiled eggs, coarsely chopped**
**1/2 cup mayonnaise**
**2 tablespoons cider vinegar**
**1 tablespoon Dijon mustard**
**1/2 teaspoon salt**

Cook potatoes in boiling water 25 minutes or until they are fork tender; drain and cool completely. Peel and cut potatoes into 1/2-inch cubes. Combine potatoes, onion, green pepper, celery, relish, and eggs in a large bowl. Combine mayonnaise and remaining ingredients in a small bowl; stir with a whisk. Pour over the potato mixture, tossing gently to coat. Cover and refrigerate at least 8 hours.

*Makes 6 to 8 servings.*

# Hotlanta Slaw

This flavorful slaw is a favorite at the Hotlanta Festival in Georgia. Crunchy pecans, sweet peaches, and the sizzle of jalapeño and cayenne peppers make it a riot of flavor for your mouth and an excellent pairing for smoked or grilled meats.

**1 small head green cabbage, shredded (about 8 cups)**
**5 carrots, shredded (about 3 cups)**
**1 16-ounce can sliced peaches, drained and coarsely chopped**
**1 1/4 cups chopped toasted pecans**
**1 bunch green onions, thinly sliced (about 1 cup)**
**1 cup mayonnaise**
**1/2 cup lemon juice**
**1/2 cup cider vinegar**
**2 tablespoons poppy seeds**
**2 jalapeño peppers, seeded and minced**
**2 cloves garlic, minced**
**1 teaspoon ground black pepper**
**1 teaspoon salt**

**1 teaspoon sugar**
**1/4 teaspoon paprika**
**Pinch of cayenne pepper**

Mix together cabbage, carrots, peaches, pecans, and green onions in a large bowl; set aside.

Combine mayonnaise, lemon juice, vinegar, poppy seeds, jalapeño, garlic, black pepper, salt, sugar, paprika, and cayenne pepper. Toss with the cabbage mixture and refrigerate for at least one hour before serving to allow flavors to blend.

*Makes 12 servings.*

# Hot Slaw

Awww yeah! The party's on. Prepare this slaw and know that the "queue"—as in barbeque—will soon follow.

**5 slices of bacon, fried crisp (reserve drippings)**
**1 1/4 teaspoons sugar**
**1/4 teaspoon salt**
**1/4 teaspoon black pepper**
**3 tablespoons hot pepper vinegar**
**4 cups shredded cabbage**
**2 cups shredded purple cabbage**
**1 1/4 cups chopped tomato**
**1 1/4 cups peeled and chopped cucumber**
**3/4 cup thinly sliced green onions**

Crumble bacon and set aside. Add sugar, salt, pepper, and vinegar to the pan drippings. Stir well and cook over medium heat until the mixture comes to a boil. Combine the cabbage and remaining ingredients in a large bowl; add the vinegar dressing and toss gently to mix. Garnish with bacon and serve immediately.

*Makes 8 to 10 servings.*

# Fresh Avocado Salad

This salad first appeared on my table this summer. It received so many rave reviews that I decided to include it for your enjoyment. It's great with almost any summer food, especially grilled meats. If the ingredients look familiar, they should. It's a salad-size version of almost everyone's favorite—guacamole! To Italianize it, substitute basil or parsley for the cilantro.

**4 ripe, but slightly firm avocadoes, peeled, pitted, and quartered**
**2 vine-ripened tomatoes, washed and quartered**
**3 large cloves of garlic, minced**
**1/4 cup cilantro, finely chopped**
**1/4 cup lime juice**
**1/4 cup olive oil**
**Kosher salt**

Combine avocado, tomatoes, garlic, and cilantro in a mixing bowl and mix to blend. In a separate container combine the lime juice and olive oil; mix well and dress salad. Refrigerate to chill and add salt to taste just before serving.

*Makes 4 to 6 servings.*

# Interdenominational Theological Center

*A wise man who knows proverbs, reconciles difficulties.*
—African proverb

ON NOVEMBER 8, 1866, the board of bishops of the Methodist Episcopal Church, assembled at New York City, declared: "The emancipation of millions of slaves has opened at our very doors a wide field of calling. . . . The time may come when the states in the South will make some provision for the education of the colored children now growing up in utter ignorance in their midst. But thus far they have made none, nor perhaps can it soon be expected of them. Christian philanthropy must supply this lack. We cannot turn away from the appeal that comes home to our consciences and hearts. Nor can we delay. The emergency is upon us, and we must begin to work now."

Following the abolition of slavery, many missionaries and ministers from diverse but like-minded church denominations flocked to the South where they established churches and schools to evangelize and educate

**Atlanta Baptist Seminary, the early home of the Morehouse School of Religion, which was organized to train black Baptist ministers following emancipation.**
*(Private collection)*

former slaves. In doing so, they sought to not only educate minds, but also to convert grateful hearts to their own Christian denominations. During this period several denominations, such as the American Home Mission Society, converged on Atlanta because, as the gateway to the South, Atlanta was home to a large black populace. They established educational institutions such as Atlanta University, Clark, and Morehouse, among others, to provide secular and religious education to former slaves.

The Interdenominational Theological Center is a collection of six private Christian seminaries founded in 1958 for the purpose of training African American ministers. The schools and their denominations, in order of dates of establishment, include the following: Morehouse School of Religion, Baptist (1867); Gammon Theological Seminary, United Methodist (1883); Turner Theological Seminary, African Methodist Episcopal (1885); Phillips School of Theology, Christian Methodist Episcopal (1944); Johnson C. Smith Theological Seminary, Presbyterian USA (1867); and Charles H. Mason Theological Seminary, Church of God in Christ (1970). This unique consortium of six seminaries is a Bible-centered, social action–oriented center, proficient in the study of black religion, including churches of Africa and the Caribbean. ITC has educated more than 35 percent of all trained black ministers in the world and 50 percent of all black chaplains in the United States military, including the highest-ranking female chaplain.

Each seminary has its own dean and board of directors, and each provides for its own student financial aid and housing. This traditionally black consortium is a United Negro College Fund member and a member of the Atlanta University Center.

The ITC is located on a ten-acre plot in the heart of the Atlanta University Center. The site is a generous gift of Atlanta University. The buildings and all other facilities are modern, providing every resource for effective instruction and comfortable living.

Since its inception, the ITC has welcomed into its enrollment students from denominations other than the six constituent denominations. These students are designated as "At-Large." Currently, At-Large students make up the fourth largest of the individual student segments at the ITC and participate fully in the life of the institution.

# *Vegetables and Side Dishes*

## Sunday Collard Greens with Rice & Ham

I remember, and perhaps you do too, when collard greens were a mainstay of plates sold for $1.25 at church fund-raising dinners. Even today their heady fragrance returns me to a time when I prayed, recited my Easter "piece" before the congregation, and received spiritual and physical nurturing in my grandmother's church.

**6 to 8 cups cleaned and chopped collard leaves, loosely packed, approximately 1½ to 2 bunches**
**2 ham hocks, washed**
**2 cups cooked long-grain rice**
**1 cup coarsely chopped ham**
**Salt and pepper to taste**

Clean greens by removing thick stalks and discarding any yellowed or badly blemished leaves. Wash greens under cold running water and rinse any remaining sand from the sink. Fill sink with cold water, add greens, and plunge up and down several times to wash any remaining sand and sediment from the greens. Stack several leaves and roll cigar fashion and slice into horizontal segments slightly smaller than ¼ inch.

Place ham hocks in a large pot and add sufficient water to cover the ham hocks by 3 to 4 inches. Bring to a rapid boil. Reduce heat, cover pot, and allow ham hocks to simmer for 1½ hours, adding additional water as necessary to prevent scorching. Add the collard greens and cook until tender,

**In my parents' house, Sunday was a day of family worship.**

*(Private collection)*

approximately 1 to $1\frac{1}{2}$ hours. Young, tender greens will require less cooking time; older greens will require more cooking time. Remove all except 4 cups of "pot liquor" (liquid) and set aside. Remove ham hocks from the pot and allow to cool, so that they may be safely handled. Remove fat and skin and discard or return to the pot (depending on your dietary habits). Remove the lean meat from the bone, chop it up, and return to the pot. Add rice, ham, and additional liquid as necessary to prevent the mixture from being too dry. However, it should not be soupy. Stir to combine. Add salt and pepper to taste. Serve hot with homemade hot sauce (see recipe below) and hot corn muffins on the side.

*Makes 6 to 8 servings.*

# Hot! Hot! Hot! Homemade Hot Habañero Pepper Sauce

You almost can't serve greens in the South without passing chow-chow, a bottle of hot pepper vinegar, or some hot sauce to top them off! Your family and friends will be amazed when you present them with your own homemade hot sauce, but remember—a dab will do.

**1/2 cup chopped onion**
**3 cloves garlic, minced**
**1/2 cup chopped carrots**
**14 habañero peppers, stems and seeds removed, finely chopped**
**1 tablespoon vegetable oil**
**1/2 cup distilled vinegar**
**1/4 cup lime juice**
**Small bay leaves**

Sauté the onion and garlic in oil until the onion is limp or transparent. Next, add the carrots together with approximately 1/4 cup of water. When the water begins to boil, reduce the heat and simmer until the carrots are soft. Place the carrot mixture and peppers into a blender and purée until smooth. Don't allow the peppers to cook, since cooking dilutes the flavor of the habañero. Combine the purée with vegetable oil vinegar and lime juice, and then simmer for 5 minutes. Place a bay leaf in each sterilized jar used, add sauce, and seal.

*Makes 2 cups.*

# Garden Mustards with Fresh Red Tomatoes

As a young child visiting my grandmother in Tampa, Florida, I always attended Tyer Temple United Methodist Church of which she was a founding member. Every Sunday, my cousin Victoria and I sang in the youth choir. . . . Ok, ok, so Vicky sang and I was asked to "simply move my lips." I wasn't offended; I simply continued the exercise at Sunday dinner where my grandmother served one of her delicious greens dishes.

**3 pounds mustard greens, cleaned and chopped**
**2 ham hocks**
**8 cups water**
**2 teaspoons vegetable oil**
**2¼ cups chopped onion**
**3 cloves garlic, minced**
**2 cups peeled, seeded, and diced ripe tomatoes**
**½ teaspoon red pepper flakes**
**Salt and freshly ground pepper to taste**

Clean greens by removing thick stalks and discarding any yellowed or badly blemished leaves. Wash greens under cold running water and rinse any remaining sand from the sink. Fill sink with cold water, add greens, and plunge up and down several times to wash any remaining sand and sediment from the greens. The curly leaves of mustard greens tend to retain sand so several washings may be necessary. Stack several leaves, roll cigar fashion and slice into horizontal segments slightly smaller than ¼ inch.

Combine ham hocks and water in large pot. Place on medium-high heat. Bring to a boil. Reduce heat and simmer for about 1½ hours, or until liquid has reduced to about 3 cups. Add greens, cover, and simmer for 30 minutes. Remove cover and simmer for an additional 30 to 45 minutes or more.

Heat vegetable oil in large skillet over medium heat. Add onion and garlic. Sauté the onion for 10 minutes or until it is transparent and then stir it into the collard greens. Stir in tomatoes and red pepper flakes and cook an additional 5 to 10 minutes. Add salt and pepper to taste. Serve piping hot with a large wedge of buttermilk cornbread and cucumbers and vinegar on the side.

*Makes 4 to 6 servings.*

# Blazing Jalapeño & Turkey Greens

This is equally at home as either a one-pot Sunday meal or a side dish.

**5 pounds assorted greens (collard, kale, mustard, and turnip, etc.)**
**2 tablespoons vegetable oil**
**1 large onion, chopped**
**1/2 cup green bell pepper, chopped**
**3 jalapeño peppers, seeded and minced (optional)**
**1 quart chicken broth**
**2 smoked turkey wings, approximately 2 to 2 1/2 pounds**
**Seasoned salt and ground black pepper to taste**
**Chopped fresh jalapeño peppers**
**Chopped onions**

Clean greens by removing thick stalks and discarding any yellowed or badly blemished leaves. Wash greens under cold running water and rinse any remaining sand from the sink. Fill sink with cold water, add greens, and plunge up and down several times to wash any remaining sand and sediment from the greens. The curly leaves of mustard greens tend to retain sand so several washings may be necessary. Roll leaves cigar fashion and slice into horizontal segments slightly smaller than 1/4 inch.

In a large pot, combine the vegetable oil, onions, green bell pepper, and jalapeños; sauté over medium heat until the onions are limp. Add chicken broth and smoked turkey wings; bring to a rapid boil over high heat. Reduce heat, cover, and simmer for 1 hour. Add additional broth as necessary to prevent scorching. Gradually stir in the greens, allowing each batch to wilt before adding more greens. Bury the turkey wings in the simmering greens.

Cover and reduce the heat to medium-low. Continue cooking the greens an additional 30 minutes. Uncover the pot and cook an additional 15 to 30 minutes, or until the greens are tender to personal taste, stirring occasionally. Younger greens will require less cooking time; older greens will require more. Remove the turkey wings. Discard the skin and bones, chop the meat, and return to the pot. Season with seasoned salt and pepper to taste.

Using a slotted spoon, transfer the greens to a serving dish. Serve hot with additional chopped peppers and onion on the side for garnish.

A chunk of cornbread and some sliced tomatoes with onions would make this meal a feast by anyone's definition.

*Makes 6 to 8 servings.*

# Collard Greens & Cabbage with Sweet Onion Relish

What a tasty dish; especially when served with down-home chicken and a skillet of pan bread! Today it seems to be calling my name . . . maybe this Sunday?

**3 slices of bacon**
**1 large onion, chopped**
**1 large green pepper, seeded and chopped**
**3 large cloves of garlic, peeled and chopped**
**2 medium ham hocks**
**4 bunches collard greens, cleaned and cut**
**1 head cabbage, cleaned and cut up**
**1/4 teaspoon crushed red peppers or to taste**
**Salt and pepper to taste**

Place bacon in a large stockpot and fry over medium high heat to render fat. Continue to cook the bacon until it is slightly browned. Add onion, pepper, and garlic and sauté until the onion is limp or transparent. Add the ham hocks, cover with water by 2 to 3 inches or more to allow the ham

**Sunday dinner, fragrant and inviting, greeted you warmly at the front door, drew you in with a smile, and wrapped its arms around you.**

*(Private collection)*

hocks to boil freely. Place on medium-high heat. Bring to a boil. Reduce heat and simmer for about 1½ hours. Add the collard greens; cover and cook until tender, approximately 1 hour or to taste. Add the cabbage during the last 20 minutes of cooking time and cook until tender or to taste. Season with salt and pepper to taste. Offer sweet onion relish to garnish (recipe follows).

*Makes 10 to 12 servings.*

# Sweet Onion Relish

**10 pounds Vidalia onions, peeled and quartered**
**½ cup salt**
**1 quart cider vinegar**
**1 teaspoon turmeric**

**1 teaspoon pickling spice**
**1 4-ounce jar chopped pimento**
**4½ cups sugar**

Process onions in a food processor to yield 1½ gallons. Add salt and allow to stand for 30 minutes. Squeeze juice from the onions and discard; place onions in a large pot. Add vinegar. Place spices in cheese cloth or tea ball. Add spice ball and sugar to the vinegar. Bring mixture to a boil and simmer for 30 minutes, stirring often. Spoon onions and sufficient liquid to cover into canning jars, which have been sterilized according to manufacturer's directions, leaving ½ inch headspace. Remove air bubbles by running a plastic knife to the bottom of the jar several times. Tighten lids and process in a water canner according to manufacturer's directions or for 10 minutes in a boiling water bath.

*Makes 8 pints.*

# Boiled String Beans with Pig's Tails

Before purchasing string or green beans check for freshness by breaking a bean in half. The bean should snap crisply and have a flavorful taste with just a hint of sweetness. Never select beans that are dull, limp, and flat-tasting.

**8 pig's tails**
**2⅓ pounds fresh string beans**
**½ cup chopped onion**
**2½ teaspoons salt**
**1 teaspoon black pepper**
**1 teaspoon sugar**

Place pig's tails in a large pot with sufficient water to cover the pig's tails by 3 to 4 inches. Bring to a rapid boil over high heat. Reduce heat, cover, and simmer for 1 hour. Add additional water as necessary to prevent scorching. Prepare the green beans while the pig's tails are simmering. Snap the stem at each end of the bean, without severing it from the bean; then pull gently along the length of the bean to remove the string and the stem. (It may not be necessary to remove the string from very young beans.) Rinse the beans in a colander under cold running water and drain. Add the beans and remaining ingredients to the pot and allow to simmer until the beans are tender, 30 to 45 minutes or to taste. Add more seasoning according to taste.

*Makes 4 large servings.*

# Pole Beans

Nothing beats the taste of garden fresh pole beans. In the middle of winter, I sometimes find myself counting the days until summer when my garden will again produce pole beans! Pole beans are the broad, flat, thick-skinned cousin of conventional string or green beans and they are ideal for slow cooking. In my family we are guilty of slow cooking all beans grouped in this category. However, pole beans simply must be slow cooked.

**1 smoked ham hock**
**3 pounds pole beans**
**1 small yellow onion, finely chopped**
**1 clove garlic, minced**
**1/2 teaspoon sugar**
**Salt and freshly ground black pepper**
**Pepper vinegar (recipe follows)**
**1/2 teaspoon cayenne pepper**

Place the ham hock in a large pot and add sufficient water to cover by 3 to 4 inches. Place over medium-high heat and bring to a boil. Reduce heat and simmer for about 1 1/2 hours. Prepare the green beans while the ham hock is simmering. Snap the stem at each end of the bean without severing it from the bean, then pull gently along the length of the bean to remove the string and the stem. (It may not be necessary to remove the string from very young beans.) Rinse the beans in a colander under cold running water and drain. Add the beans and remaining ingredients to the pot and allow the beans to simmer until tender, 45 to 60 minutes or to taste. Add additional seasoning according to taste.

Serve hot with condiments such as chopped raw onion, pickled hot peppers, and pepper vinegar.

*Makes 10 to 12 servings.*

### PEPPER VINEGAR

My grandfather made his pepper vinegar by pouring about one-fourth of the vinegar out of a cider-vinegar bottle and filling the remaining space with hot peppers from his bush in the yard. He then would allow the peppers to marinate a week or two before serving. As the pepper vinegar was used, he would simply add more vinegar. Just before the peppers became too weak for reuse, he would start another batch. Don't wait too long, though, this vinegar is addicting. You will find yourself using it on greens and other vegetables. If, like me, you don't have a pepper bush, try using small Serrano peppers, but keep in mind they are very hot and you may need fewer of them, or you can divide the batch and dilute it by adding more vinegar.

*Makes about 4 cups.*

## Sautéed Green Beans

This excellent recipe is one handed down by my grandmother to my mother and then to me. It's as treasured as any heirloom received from them.

**2 tablespoons bacon fat**
**2 pounds green beans, cleaned and tips removed**

**1 small onion, finely chopped**
**1/2 cup water**
**1 teaspoon sugar or to taste**

Heat the bacon fat in a large cooking pot. Add the beans, salt, and pepper. Sauté the beans until they are lightly golden, about 3 minutes. Add the onion and sauté another minute. Add just enough water for moisture. Stir in sugar, cover, reduce heat to medium, and cook 20 to 25 minutes or until beans are the desired tenderness. Add additional water as necessary to prevent scorching. Uncover and cook beans down for an additional 10 to 15 minutes or to taste.

*Makes 6 to 8 servings.*

**Every Sunday was also a homecoming celebration when extended family members gathered to share a meal and the traditions that bound us together.**
*(Private collection)*

# Savory Green Beans

**1½ pounds fresh green beans**
**3 tablespoons of bacon drippings or vegetable oil**
**2 cloves garlic, crushed**
**¼ cup chopped onion**
**½ teaspoon sugar**
**¼ teaspoon beef bouillon granules**
**¼ teaspoon black pepper**

Wash the green beans, trim ends, and remove the strings. Place the bacon drippings or vegetable oil in a large saucepan and sauté the garlic and onions over medium-high heat. Remove and discard the garlic. Add the remaining ingredients, cover, and cook over medium heat for 30 minutes or until the green beans reach the desired degree of tenderness.

*Makes 6 servings.*

# Baked Okra, Corn & Tomato Casserole

You can almost hear the back screen door slam, the fan humming, chairs scraping against the broom-scrubbed hardwood floor, and red Kool-Aid being poured. Amen?

**3 cups sliced fresh okra**
**⅓ cup chopped Canadian bacon**
**1 large tomato, chopped**
**½ cup frozen corn**
**1 large onion, thinly sliced**
**½ teaspoon salt**
**¼ teaspoon pepper**
**2 tablespoons water**

Preheat oven to 350°F. Coat a 1¾ quart casserole dish with a thin layer of butter. Layer half of the okra, Canadian bacon, tomato, corn, and onion slices. Sprinkle evenly with half of the salt and pepper. Repeat and sprinkle with water. Cover with aluminum foil, place in preheated oven, and bake until the vegetables are tender, 40 to 45 minutes.

*Makes 6 servings.*

# Fresh Corn, Okra & Tomato

Savor this Southern summertime tradition. When selecting fresh corn, look for fresh green husks, dry silks, and even rows of plump kernels. If you pop a kernel between your fingers and the milk is watery, the corn is immature. If it is thick and starchy, the corn is old.

**3 tablespoons butter**
**3/4 cup chopped green pepper**
**1 1/4 cups chopped onion**
**1 3/4 cups white corn cut from the cob (approximately 4 ears)**
**3/4 cup water**
**2 medium tomatoes, peeled, seeded, and chopped**
**1 3/4 tablespoons tomato paste**
**1/2 teaspoon salt**
**1/4 teaspoon ground black pepper**
**Pinch ground nutmeg**
**1/4 teaspoon paprika**
**1 1/2 cups sliced okra**

Melt butter in a large skillet over medium-high heat. Add green pepper and onion and sauté until the vegetables are crisp-tender. Reduce the heat to medium, add the corn, water, tomato, tomato paste, salt, pepper, nutmeg, and paprika; cover and continue to cook 10 minutes, stirring occasionally. Add okra, cover, and simmer 5 to 7 additional minutes. Add salt and pepper to taste.

*Makes 6 servings.*

# Fried Corn

When storing fresh corn, leave it in husks and refrigerate to prevent the sugar from turning to starch.

**12 ears fresh white corn**
**1/2 cup butter**
**2 tablespoons bacon drippings**
**1/2 cup chopped onion**
**3/4 cup water**
**1/8 teaspoon ground nutmeg**
**1/2 teaspoon salt**
**1/4 teaspoon black pepper**

Husk and remove the silk from the corn. Cut corn from the cob; forcefully scrape each cob again to remove the milk, and set aside. Combine the butter and bacon drippings in a large skillet over medium-high heat. Add onions and sauté until the onions are tender and translucent. Add corn, stir, and continue to cook for 2 to 3 minutes. Add the water, nutmeg, salt, and pepper. Cook uncovered over medium heat until the mixture comes to a boil. Reduce heat and simmer 10 to 12 minutes or until the liquid is absorbed, stirring frequently.

*Makes 10 to 12 servings.*

# Fresh Corn Fritters

**1 pint grated fresh corn, uncooked**
**1/2 cup corn milk (scraped from the cobs)**
**2 egg yolks (reserve whites)**
**1/2 cup flour**
**1 teaspoon salt**
**1 teaspoon baking powder**
**1 tablespoon melted butter**

**Sunny Sunday afternoons also bring back memories of family car rides, even when Dad was stationed overseas. (My mother is to the left, I am in the middle, and that's my Uncle Johnny on the right. Dad is taking the photo with his brand new Kodak camera.) Note the car plates.**

*(Private collection)*

Place fresh grated corn in a large mixing bowl and set aside. In a separate bowl, collect milk from cobs by forcefully scraping them with a spoon or butter knife. Measure ½ cup of the corn milk and add to the grated corn. Add the egg yolks and mix well. Next, combine flour, salt, and baking powder, mix until well blended. Add flour mixture and butter to the corn mixture and mix to combine. Beat reserved egg whites until stiff and fold into the corn mixture. Drop fritter batter from a tablespoon onto a well-greased, hot griddle or frying pan and cook like pancakes. Serve with melted butter, syrup, and plenty of crispy, fried bacon.

*Makes 6 servings.*

# Fresh Butter Beans

**3 tablespoons bacon drippings or 4 slices bacon**
**1 large onion, finely chopped**
**1 cloves garlic, minced**
**1 meaty ham hock**

Heat bacon drippings in a large pot over medium-high heat or render drippings from bacon and reserve bacon. Add onion and garlic and sauté until the onion is translucent. Rinse ham hock and place it in the pot with sufficient water to cover. Bring ham hock to a rapid boil, reduce heat to low, cover, and simmer for one hour. Rinse beans before adding them to the pot. Bring to a boil. Reduce heat and simmer, stirring occasionally, until beans are tender, 30 to 45 minutes. Add more water as needed to prevent scorching. Cut ham from the ham hock, chop, and return the meat to the pot. Crumble reserved bacon and serve as an optional garnish for the beans.

*Makes 6 to 8 servings.*

# Spicy Hot Pinto Beans

Spicy hot and deliciously satisfying!

**1 pound dried pinto beans**
**2 ham hocks**
**2 tablespoons bacon drippings or five slices of bacon**
**1 large onion, diced**
**3/4 cup chopped green pepper**
**5 garlic cloves, finely minced**
**1 jalapeño pepper, stemmed, seeded, and finely chopped**
**1/4 cup Worcestershire sauce**
**1 pound smoked link sausage, cut into 12-inch slices**
**1/4 cup firmly packed brown sugar**
**2 tablespoons ground cumin**
**1 tablespoon chili powder**

**1 teaspoon black pepper**
**1 teaspoon hot pepper sauce**
**1 teaspoon salt**
**2 small bay leaves**
**1 16-ounce can undrained, chopped tomatoes**

Pick over beans and remove any stones or other foreign objects. Rinse beans and place them in a large non-reactive container with sufficient water to cover by 2 inches and soak overnight. Rinse ham hocks and place them in a large Dutch oven with sufficient water to cover by 3 to 4 inches. Bring ham hocks to a rapid boil, reduce heat to low, cover, and simmer for one hour. Drain the beans and rinse again before adding them to the Dutch oven.

Heat bacon drippings in a large skillet over medium-high heat or render drippings from the bacon and discard bacon. Add onion, green pepper, garlic, and jalapeño pepper to the drippings and sauté until the onion is translucent and the remaining vegetables are tender. Add to the beans. Add Worcestershire and the remaining ingredients except the tomatoes; bring the mixture to a rapid boil, reduce heat, cover and simmer for 2 hours or until the beans are tender, stirring occasionally. Add tomatoes and juice. Cook an additional 30 minutes. Cut lean meat from the ham hock, chop, and return the meat to the pot. Remove bay leaves before serving.

*Makes 10 servings.*

# Black-Eyed Peas and Tomatoes

Dried peas and beans, both rich in nutrients, provide much needed sustenance to people during the winter months when fresh beans and vegetables are too expensive. However, they require soaking to rehydrate. If an overnight soaking is impossible, there is a quicker method: Combine 1 pound dried peas or beans and 2 quarts of water in a large pot and bring to a boil. Place a cover on the pot and cook an additional two minutes before removing the peas from the heat and allowing them to stand 1 hour. Drain, and then cook according to directions.

**1 pound black-eyed peas**
**2 tablespoons bacon drippings or vegetable oil**
**1 large onion, chopped**
**1 green pepper, stemmed, seeded, and chopped**
**1 clove garlic, finely minced**
**2 large meaty ham hocks**
**2 bay leaves**
**1 teaspoon salt**
**1½ cups garden fresh chopped tomatoes, undrained**

Pick over beans and remove any stones or other foreign objects. Rinse beans and place them in a large non-reactive container with sufficient water to cover by 2 inches and soak overnight. Place bacon drippings or vegetable oil in a large Dutch oven and bring to medium heat. Add onions, green pepper, and garlic to Dutch oven. Cook until onions are transparent. Rinse ham hocks and place them in the Dutch oven with sufficient water to cover. Increase heat to medium-high and bring ham hocks to a rapid boil, reduce heat to low, cover, and simmer for one hour. Drain the beans and rinse again before adding them to the Dutch oven. Add bay leaves and salt, bring beans to a rapid boil, reduce heat, cover, and simmer 2 hours or until the beans are tender. Remove top and cook an additional 20 minutes uncovered to allow the beans to cook down. Add the tomatoes, stir, and cook an additional 15 to 20 minutes.

*Makes 6 to 8 servings.*

# Black-Eyed Peas with Smoked Pork

Pass the peas and praise the Lord!

**1 pound dried black-eyed peas, rinsed, picked over, soaked overnight**
**1 smoked pork picnic shoulder, about 5 to 7 pounds**
**2 bay leaves**
**Salt and pepper to taste**

Pick over the peas to remove any foreign objects and soak overnight in sufficient water to cover by 2 to 3 inches. Place pork in a large pot of boiling water, cover, and bring to a second boil. Reduce heat, add bay leaves, and simmer for 1½ hours. Drain and rinse the peas and add to the pot, and simmer an additional 1½ hours longer, or until pork and peas are tender. Remove pork from pot; trim off skin and fat layers. Slice about half of the pork ¼ inch thick. Season peas with salt and pepper to taste and allow the peas to cook down until liquid reaches the desired consistency. Serve with pork slices, rice, and corn bread.

*Makes 6 to 8 servings.*

**Sunday was a day to relax and recreate. Sometimes—after church, of course—the entire family picnicked and fished.**

*(Private collection)*

# John's Hip-Hoppin' Black-Eyed Peas

Black-eyed peas, thought to have originated in North Africa, were probably introduced to the New World by Spanish explorers and African slaves. Now common in the Southern United States, they are available dried, fresh, canned, and frozen.

**1 pound dried black-eyed peas**
**1 large onion, peeled and coarsely chopped**
**1 large green pepper, seeded and chopped**
**3 jalapeño peppers, seeded and chopped**
**3 cloves garlic, large**
**3 tablespoons vegetable oil**
**2 smoked ham hocks**
**2 bay leaves**
**3 teaspoons seasoned salt**
**1/2 teaspoon onion powder**
**1/2 teaspoon ground cumin**
**3/4 teaspoon dried thyme leaves**
**1 1/2 cups seeded and diced tomatoes**

Pick over the peas to remove any foreign objects and soak overnight in sufficient water to cover by 2 to 3 inches. In a large pot, sauté the onions, green pepper, jalapeño pepper and garlic in the vegetable oil until the onion is limp or transparent. Rinse the ham hocks, add to the pot, also adding sufficient water to cover by 3 to 4 inches. Place on medium-high heat and bring to a boil. Reduce heat and simmer for about 1 1/2 hours. Drain and rinse the peas, add to the pot, and simmer an additional 1 hour. Add the bay leaves, seasoned salt, onion powder, ground cumin, and dried thyme leaves. Remove the ham hocks, coarsely chop the lean meat, and return it to the pot. Add the tomatoes and cook down an additional half hour or until the beans are soft and the liquid slightly thickened.

*Makes 4 to 6 servings.*

# Butter Beans & Okra

I love all types of beans, prepared in a variety of ways. Butter beans, also known as calico beans or Madagascar beans, are among my favorites.

**1½ pounds dried butter beans**
**1 meaty ham bone or 3 large ham hocks**
**3 cups water**
**½ pound okra, washed and thinly sliced**
**2 tablespoons solid vegetable shortening**
**1 tablespoon sugar**
**1 tablespoon salt**
**2 teaspoons freshly ground black pepper**

Pick over the beans to remove any foreign objects and soak overnight in sufficient water to cover by 2 to 3 inches. In a large pot combine hambone or ham hocks and sufficient water to cover by 3 to 4 inches. Place on medium-high heat and bring to a boil. Reduce heat and simmer for about 1½ hours. Remove the ham hocks from the pot and set aside to cool. Meanwhile, drain and rinse the beans and add them to the pot. Cover and allow the beans to simmer for an additional hour. While the beans are simmering, remove the lean meat from the cooled ham hocks, shred it, and return the shredded meat to the pot. Add the okra, cover, and simmer an additional 25 minutes. Uncover the pot and cook down an additional 15 to 20 minutes or until the beans are tender and the liquid is slightly thickened.

*Makes 6 to 8 large servings.*

# Twice-Baked Honey & Pecan Sweet Potatoes

**6 medium sweet potatoes, scrubbed**
**3 tablespoons butter**
**3 tablespoons honey**
**$^1/_4$ teaspoon salt**
**$^1/_4$ cup pecans, toasted and chopped**

Preheat oven to 400°F. Prick each potato once with a fork and bake it on a foil lined, rimmed baking sheet 45 to 55 minutes or until it is fork-tender and soft. Remove the potatoes from the oven and set aside to cool. When

**And then there was Easter Sunday with cousins Deborah, Judy, and Barbara Jeane Quick.**
*(Private collection)*

they are sufficiently cool to handle, cut them in half lengthwise and scoop insides into a medium bowl. Mash together with the next three ingredients until smooth. Spoon potatoes back into skins and garnish with the pecans. Reduce oven temperature to 350°F. Place the potatoes on a foil-lined baking sheet and bake uncovered for 15 minutes.

*Makes 6 servings.*

# Sweet Potato Casserole

**3 cups grated uncooked sweet potato**
**1 1/4 cups sugar**
**1 cup table cream**
**1/2 teaspoon vanilla extract**
**1/4 cup butter**
**4 eggs, slightly beaten**
**3 tablespoons all-purpose flour**
**1/4 teaspoon allspice**
**1/2 teaspoon ground nutmeg**
**1/4 teaspoon ground cinnamon**

Preheat oven to 350°F. Lightly butter a shallow, 2-quart baking dish and set aside. Combine the above ingredients and mix well before spooning into the prepared casserole dish. Bake uncovered for 30 minutes. Stir and bake an additional 15 minutes or until a knife inserted in the center comes out clean.

*Makes 6 to 8 servings.*

# Candied Yams with Bourbon

Simply delicious!

**6 to 8 large sweet potatoes, peeled, boiled, and cubed**
**1/4 cup light corn syrup**
**1/4 cup dark corn syrup**
**3 tablespoons brown sugar**
**1 teaspoon cinnamon**
**1/4 cup good Kentucky bourbon**
**Chopped pecans, toasted**

Arrange sweet potatoes in a buttered casserole pan or dish. Combine remaining ingredients and pour over potatoes. Bake at 350°F until bubbling hot. Garnish with toasted pecans.

*Makes 4 to 6 servings.*

# Sweet Potato Soufflé

Can it be Sunday dinner without sweet potatoes? I don't think so, and neither will you once you try this sweetly delicious soufflé.

**3 cups cooked sweet potatoes, mashed**
**1/2 cup sugar**
**1/4 cup melted butter**
**1/2 cup light corn syrup**
**3 eggs**
**1/4 teaspoon nutmeg**
**1 1/4 teaspoons vanilla extract**

Spray a 2-quart baking dish with cooking spray. Preheat oven to 350°F. Mash sweet potatoes and set aside. Combine sugar, butter, syrup, eggs, nutmeg, and vanilla. Beat until creamy. Stir butter mixture into mashed sweet potatoes. Pour potato mixture into prepared dish. Prepare topping (recipe follows) and sprinkle over potatoes. Bake the soufflé in a preheated oven for 35 minutes or until soufflé is lightly browned.

*Makes 6 to 8 servings.*

### TOPPING

**1 cup brown sugar, firmly packed**
**1/2 cup butter**
**1/2 cup flour**
**1/2 teaspoon cinnamon**
**1 cup chopped pecans**

Combine brown sugar, butter, flour, cinnamon, and chopped nuts. Sprinkle over Sweet Potato Soufflé before baking.

**Easter Sunday with my cousins and brother Kevin (note the 45 rpm records behind Kevin).**
*(Private collection)*

# Old-Fashioned Parsley Mashed Potatoes

The rich, old fashioned flavor of this potato dish hearkens to an earlier era when dinner took time to prepare and diners lingered over their meals while sharing memories and traditions.

**8 medium white potatoes, peeled and cubed**
**1 medium onion, finely chopped**
**Up to 2/3 cup of evaporated milk, divided**
**1/3 cup butter**
**1 teaspoon salt**
**1/4 teaspoon sugar**
**1/8 teaspoon white pepper**
**2 tablespoons finely minced parsley**

Cook the potatoes and onion in enough boiling water to cover for 15 minutes or until the potatoes are fork-tender. Drain the water away, retaining the onion with the potatoes, add remaining ingredients and mash with additional milk as needed until the potatoes reach their desired consistency. Serve piping hot. With gravy or not, these potatoes are delicious either way.

*Makes 8 servings.*

# Three-Cheese Macaroni 'n' Cheese

Mac and cheese is another Sunday favorite in my family. How about yours?

**1 pound elbow macaroni**
**1/4 stick butter**
**8 ounces mild Cheddar cheese, grated**
**8 ounces Colby Jack cheese, grated**
**2 cups grated Monterey Jack cheese**
**1/4 cup table cream**

**1/4 cup sour cream**
**Pinch of nutmeg**
**Salt and pepper to taste**

Preheat oven to 350°F. Cook macaroni according to package directions; drain, and add butter and cheese. Stir gently to combine. Add table cream, sour cream, and nutmeg. Continue cooking until cheeses are melted and the mixture is smooth and creamy. Stir constantly to prevent scorching. Add salt and pepper to taste. Pour mixture into a lightly buttered baking dish and bake for approximately 15 minutes.

*Makes 4 to 6 servings.*

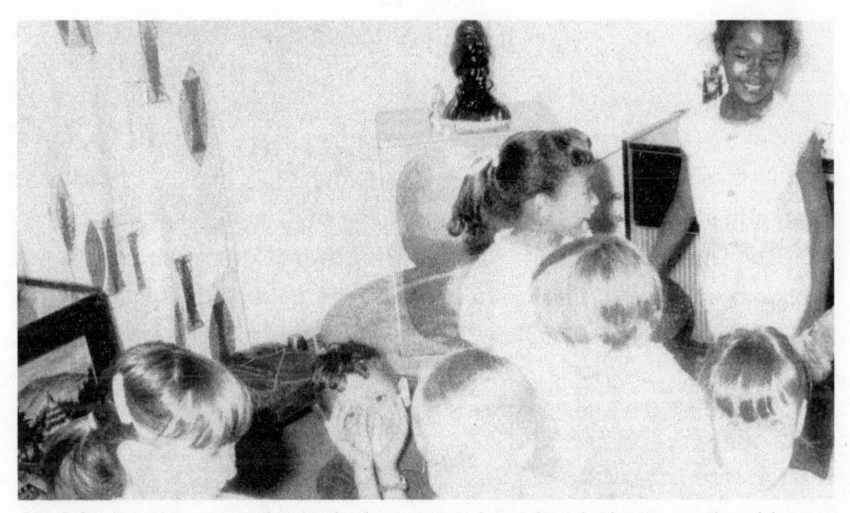

**Birthday Sundays were always the best. I am the girl with the ponytail and bangs, standing excitedly near the stereo and waiting to do the twist.**

*(Private collection)*

# Easy Jamaican Rice & Peas

I first tasted Jamaican beans and rice when researching this book in Atlanta. It was love at first taste. I hope you will feel the same!

Fresh gungo peas, otherwise known as "pigeon peas," are used when in season, but dried red beans are usually the "peas" in Jamaican rice and peas—probably one of the island's best loved and most exported dishes!

**1 19-ounce can kidney beans, reserve liquid**
**2 cups coconut milk**
**2 cloves minced garlic**
**5 green onions, chopped (approximately 1/2 cup)**
**1 jalapeño pepper, seeded and minced**
**3/4 teaspoon dried thyme**
**1/2 teaspoon salt**
**1/2 teaspoon black pepper**
**2 cups rice**
**1 tablespoon butter**

Combine the liquid from the canned peas with the coconut milk, and add additional water, if necessary, to make 3 1/2 cups of liquid. Pour the liquid into a large saucepan and add the peas, minced garlic, green onions, jalapeño pepper, thyme, salt, and black pepper. Bring to a rolling boil and boil for 3 minutes. Add the rice and butter and stir once. Reduce the heat to low, cover, and simmer for 20 to 30 minutes or until all the liquid is completely absorbed and the rice is cooked. (If the rice is not tender after the water evaporates, add 2 to 4 tablespoons of water, cover, and simmer for another 5 to 10 minutes.)

*Makes 4 to 6 servings.*

# Ethiopian Lentils

Among the plethora of ethnic restaurants dotting Atlanta's culinary landscape are a number of Ethiopian restaurants. Lentils are served at most. They appeal to my Southern heritage, and in fact, to me they are just another delicious bean.

**2 red onions, chopped**
**3 cloves garlic, minced**
**1/4 cup ghee (recipe follows)**
**6 cups water or chicken broth**
**6 cups mild green chilies, roasted, peeled, seeded and chopped**
**2 1/4 tablespoons Berbere Spice Mix (recipe follows)**
**1 pound lentils**
**Freshly ground black pepper**

In a 4-quart pot, sauté the onion and garlic in the ghee until the onions are tender. Add the broth, bring to a boil, and simmer 10 minutes. Add chilies and Berbere Spice Mix. Add the lentils and cook covered for another 35 to 40 minutes, or until most of liquid is absorbed. Add additional broth as necessary to prevent sticking. Season with ground black pepper to taste.

This dish is especially delicious when served with brown rice and sliced fresh tomatoes.

*Makes 6 to 8 servings.*

# Ghee

Ghee is basically clarified butter. It's very tasty and excellent for cooking!

**1 pound unsalted butter**
**4 whole cloves**

Place butter in a heavy, medium-size pan and melt over medium heat. Reduce heat and continue to cook until the butter begins to foam and whitish curds begin to form on the bottom of the pot. Keep a close watch on the ghee, as it can easily burn. At this point add your cloves and stir. The cloves aid in clarifying the butter. If it turns brown, or has a nutty flavor, it is burned and must be discarded.

Spoon away the foam to see if the butter is clear. Some people save the foam for use in cooking vegetables or making Indian bread; otherwise, it can be discarded. At this point the butter will smell like popcorn and should be turning a lovely golden color and clearing. Once the ghee has stopped foaming and is clear all the way to the bottom of the pan it is done. Remove from the heat and spoon away any remaining foam. Allow it to sit until it is just warm and then pour it through a fine sieve or layers of cheesecloth into a clean, dry glass container with a tight lid. Discard the curds at the bottom of the saucepan. Each pound of butter requires approximately 15 minutes of cooking time.

*Note:* Because ghee contains no milk solids, it can be kept safely without refrigeration for an extended period of time. However, be very cautious to keep water out of the stored ghee because bacteria can readily grow in the combination of these liquids.

*Makes 2 cups.*

# Berbere Spice Mix (Ethiopian Hot Pepper Seasoning)

This spice mix is used in many Ethiopian dishes. Make extra; you'll soon find yourself using it in other recipes as well.

**1 teaspoon ground ginger**
**1/4 teaspoon ground cinnamon**
**3/4 teaspoon ground cardamom**
**1/4 teaspoon ground allspice**
**1/2 teaspoon ground coriander**
**1/4 teaspoon turmeric**

**2 tablespoons salt**
**1 tablespoon ground fenugreek**
**1¼ cups cayenne pepper**
**2½ tablespoons sweet Hungarian pepper**
**½ teaspoon nutmeg**

Combine the spices in a small frying pan and toast over medium-low heat for approximately 2 minutes while stirring constantly. Remove from the pan and cool for 5 minutes. Store spice mix in a tightly covered jar.

*Makes about 1½ cups.*

**Even in the face of adversity and oppression, fathers looked toward the future as they loved, guided, and provided for their families.**

*(Private collection)*

# Berbere Sauce (Ethiopian Hot Sauce)

This North African sauce is named after the Berbers, a tribe noted for their horsemanship. Hot pepper sauce as a flavor enhancer is offered by almost every culture. I hope you will enjoy this delicious offering from Africa.

**1 teaspoon turmeric**
**1/2 teaspoon garlic powder**
**1/2 teaspoon ground cloves**
**Mexican dried chilies, seeded**
**2 teaspoons cumin**
**1/2 teaspoon cardamom**
**1/2 teaspoon black peppercorns**
**1/4 teaspoon allspice**
**1/2 teaspoon fenugreek**
**5 ounces red Mexican dried chilies, seeds removed**
**2 teaspoons salt**
**1 teaspoon ground ginger**
**1/2 teaspoon ground nutmeg**
**1/2 cup dried onions**
**1/2 cup salad oil**
**1/2 cup red wine**
**Cayenne powder**

Toast the spices, chilies, and salt in a hot skillet, shaking constantly, for a couple of minutes, until they start to crackle and pop. Grind or process the spices and dried onion to form a powder. Place the spice blend in a bowl and add the oil and wine. Add cayenne to taste. Stir until thickened and store in a covered plastic container in the refrigerator.

*Makes about 2 1/2 cups.*

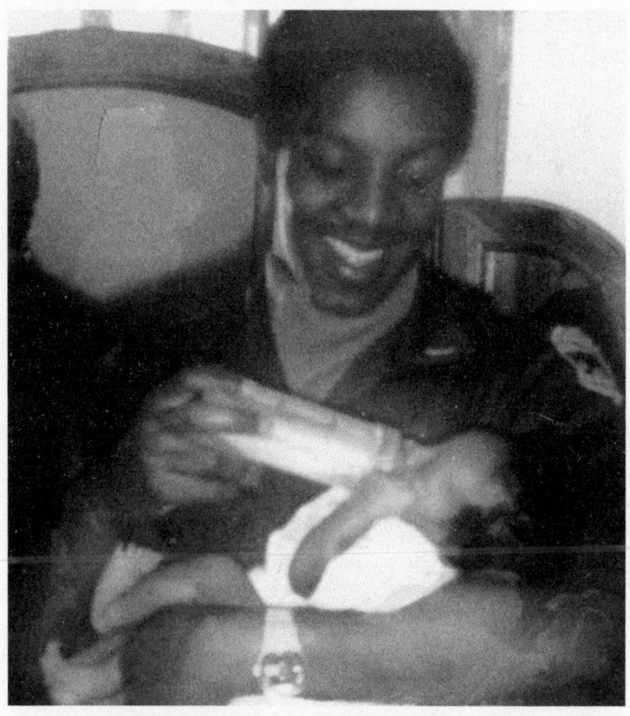

This tradition of unity, love, and strength continues to be handed down in my own family. For that I very gratefully give thanks.

*(Private collection)*

# Morehouse School of Medicine

*There is no medicine to cure hatred.*
—African proverb

## Morehouse: A Small Medical School with Outrageous Ambition!

UNTIL CHALLENGED BY civil rights activists, hospitals in the North and South were racially segregated. By 1923, about 200 black hospitals had been founded, three-fourths of them in the South, but they were under white control. Only six provided internships, and none had residency programs. One black hospital, McVicar, a department of Spelman Seminary, was considered outstanding, but it too was under white control. Black doctors, even those with excellent credentials from Howard, Meherry, Harvard, or Rush, could not enter city hospital practices until 1953 and were not admitted to many Southern and some Northern medical societies. Under these conditions it was difficult for doctors to obtain the practical experience required for professional growth and excellence. Those African-American doctors fortunate enough to have a practice of their own could not admit a patient to McVicar's segregated facilities without permission from a white doctor.

The NAACP and other civil rights organizations sought legal remedies and AUC students protested at the segregated hospitals to draw national attention to the problems experienced by black Americans when seeking medical care. As legal battles were fought to extend the holding in *Brown v. Board of Education* to hospital desegregation cases, community activist Xerona Clayton coordinated the activities of Atlanta's black doctors in the Doctors' Committee for Implementation project, which resulted in the desegregation of all of Atlanta's hospitals. But some of the earliest and perhaps, in one way, the most important support came at a time when it was least popular to support black political causes. In the 1940s Margaret Mitchell, the author of *Gone with the Wind,* worked behind the scenes with Dr. Benjamin Mays, president of Morehouse College, to anonymously provide scholarships to Morehouse students. The desegregation of hospitals opened new internship and residency opportunities to black medical students, which were previously closed to them as a result of racial discrimination. However, in regards to medical school admissions, they still fought for the limited "quota" or "minority" seats in medical schools sharply focused upon the medical needs of mainstream America.

In 1975 a medical school was established at Morehouse College. The principal teaching hospital for Morehouse is Grady Hospital, which serves a large percentage of the urban minority population in the metropolitan Atlanta area. Morehouse students assume up to half of the responsibility for patient care, medical education, and clinical research at Grady. The goal of the medical school was to address the shortage of physicians among minority communities. The Morehouse School of Medicine remains committed to training doctors who will work in underserved communities and research diseases that disproportionately affect minorities and the poor.

From its very beginning in 1975 under the direction of Dr. Louis W. Sullivan and other Morehouse alumni, Morehouse School of Medicine (no longer affiliated with Morehouse College) has been committed to preparing doctors for careers as primary care physicians—an area of medical practice that continues to be plagued by disparities in service to the African-American community. As part of their commitment to health care in black communities, the medical school focuses upon preventative health care aimed at preventing health care problems such as high blood pressure and diabetes, which have long plagued the black community.

In consideration of the changing times and health and dietary needs of African-American families, including my own, I have included some of my everyday recipes that are lower in fat and higher in fiber. However, on special occasions, I celebrate my heritage with Southern and soul food recipes that have sustained generations of Americans from slavery to freedom and beyond. I'm certain that as families struggled to send children to college or start a new business enterprise in Atlanta some of these recipes strengthened them and sustained them, welcoming them home from their fields of labor. These recipes, lest they be forgotten, are proudly included as well.

Also included are Caribbean recipes. Some may be surprised by their inclusion in an American soul food recipe book, but I am sure most Atlantans won't be. The plethora of Caribbean restaurants in the city, especially around the Atlanta University Center, attest to the fact that Africans formerly enslaved in the Caribbean migrated to the United States, bringing their recipes with them. Their common African roots and tasty spiciness ensured these recipes' adoption into the melting pot of African-American cooking.

## Apple Cider-Glazed Pork Tenderloin with Baked Sweet Potatoes & Granny Smith Apples

What a wonderful dish for an autumn harvest supper with family and friends!

**2 tablespoons dried rosemary, crushed**
**1 1/4 tablespoons grated orange rind**
**1 tablespoon olive oil**
**1/2 teaspoon salt**
**1/4 teaspoon freshly ground black pepper**
**7 garlic cloves, minced**
**3 1-pound pork tenderloins, trimmed**
**3 cups apple cider**
**3 whole cloves**
**2 bay leaves**
**1 cup fat-free, less-sodium chicken broth**

Combine the first 6 ingredients; rub evenly into pork. Place pork in a dish; cover and chill 2 hours or overnight.

In a large skillet, combine the cider, cloves, and bay leaves and bring to a boil over medium-high heat. Cook until reduced to 1 1/2 cups (about 10 minutes). Add the broth and bring the mixture to a second boil. Next, use a sharp knife to remove and discard any whitish silver skin and visible fat from the tenderloins. Add the pork tenderloins; cover and simmer 20 minutes or until done. Remove pork from pan and keep warm. Bring cooking liquids to a quick boil and continue to cook until the liquid is reduced to

3/4 cup, approximately 8 minutes. Strain reduced liquid through a fine sieve to remove solids. Spoon over warm thin-sliced pork and serve with Baked Sweet Potatoes and Granny Smith Apples (recipe follows).

*Makes 12 servings.*

# Baked Sweet Potatoes & Granny Smith Apples

**5 cups (1/2-inch) cubed, peeled sweet potatoes (about 1 1/2 pounds)**
**1 1/4 cups coarsely chopped onion**
**1/4 cup packed brown sugar**
**1/3 cup fresh orange juice**
**2 tablespoons vegetable oil**
**1 tablespoon fresh lemon juice**
**1/2 teaspoon salt**
**1/2 teaspoon black pepper**
**1/8 teaspoon ground nutmeg**
**3 cups (1-inch) cubed Granny Smith apples (about 1 1/4 pounds)**
**1 cup raisins**

Preheat oven to 350°F. Combine sweet potatoes and onion in a 13 × 9-inch baking dish and set aside. In a separate bowl, combine the sugar and next 6 ingredients. Pour the orange juice mixture over the sweet potato mixture; toss well. Cover with aluminum foil and bake at 350°F for 30 minutes; stir occasionally. Stir in the apples and raisins, replace foil, and bake an additional 15 minutes or until apple is tender. Uncover and bake an additional 5 minutes.

*Makes 12 to 14 servings.*

# Cumin & Sage Pork Tenderloin

**2 tablespoons dark brown sugar**
**1 teaspoon ground cumin**
**1/2 teaspoon ground sage**
**1 teaspoon coarsely ground black pepper**
**2 teaspoons cider vinegar**
**1 onion, sliced thin**
**2 large cloves garlic, minced**
**Dash of salt**
**1 1-pound pork tenderloin**
**Cooking spray**

Combine the first 7 ingredients in a zippered plastic storage bag. Shake to mix and set aside.

Next, use a sharp knife to remove and discard any whitish silver skin and visible fat from the tenderloins. Put the pork in the plastic storage bag, which contains the marinade, and place in the refrigerator for one hour, turning occasionally. Remove pork from the plastic bag and discard the marinade. Place pork on a broiler pan coated with cooking spray. Insert meat thermometer into thickest portion of pork and bake in a preheated 400°F oven for 25 minutes or until thermometer registers 160°F (slightly pink). Cut pork into thin slices before serving.

# Grilled Pork Tenderloin

**2 pork tenderloins, about 12 ounces each**
**1 tablespoon olive oil**
**1/4 teaspoon salt**
**1/8 teaspoon onion powder**
**1/8 teaspoon paprika**
**1/4 teaspoon ground sage**
**1/4 teaspoon freshly ground black pepper**

Preheat grill or broiler to medium-high. Next, use a sharp knife to remove and discard any whitish silver skin and visible fat from the tenderloins.

Rub the tenderloins with olive oil, combine seasoning ingredients, and use the mixture to generously season the tenderloin. Sear the pork on all sides on the grill or under the broiler. Lower the heat to medium and cook for 8 to 12 minutes, or until the tenderloin is just cooked through. Transfer it to a warm platter and let the meat rest for 2 to 3 minutes before slicing.

*Makes 6 to 8 servings.*

## David Satcher

**Born in Anniston, Alabama, in 1941, David Satcher graduated from Morehouse College in Atlanta in 1963 and received his M.D. and Ph.D. from Case Western Reserve University in 1970. He became the sixteenth surgeon general of the United States in 1998, and served simultaneously as assistant secretary for health. He is currently the interim president and director of the new Morehouse School of Medicine National Center for Primary Care.**

**Dr. Satcher is a former Robert Wood Johnson Clinical Scholar and Macy Faculty Fellow. He is the recipient of many honorary degrees and numerous distinguished honors, including top awards from the American Medical Association, the American College of Physicians, the American Academy of Family Physicians, and *Ebony* magazine. In 1995, he received the Breslow Award in Public Health and in 1997 the New York Academy of Medicine Lifetime Achievement Award. He also received the Bennie Mays Trailblazer Award and the Jimmy and Roslyn Carter Award for Humanitarian Contributions to the Health of Humankind from the National Foundation for Infectious Diseases.**

# Herb-Roasted Cornish Hens

**3 Cornish hens**
**Salt (or salt substitute) and freshly ground pepper to taste**
**5 cloves garlic, sliced**
**2 tablespoons fresh rosemary leaves**
**2 tablespoons minced, fresh thyme**
**1½ bay leaves**
**3 shallots, roughly chopped**
**2 carrots, roughly chopped into 1-inch pieces**
**2 stalks celery, roughly chopped into 1-inch pieces**
**1½ lemons**
**Paprika**
**Finely minced parsley**

Preheat the oven to 375°F. Wash the Cornish hens under cold running water and pat dry. Next, season with salt or salt substitute and pepper inside and out. Combine the garlic, rosemary, and thyme. Divide the mixture evenly and use it to stuff the hens. Place half a bay leaf inside each hen. Add some shallots, carrots, and celery to each hen's cavity. Spread any remaining vegetables on the bottom of a roasting pan. Place the hens on top of the vegetables and squeeze lemon juice over the hens then add half a lemon to each hen cavity. Roast in the preheated oven until the hens are golden brown and crisp and the juices run clear when the thigh is pierced with a sharp knife, approximately 45 minutes.

Transfer the hens to a warm serving platter and let rest for approximately 5 minutes. Remove the skin from the hens and cut each one in half. Garnish with paprika and parsley before serving.

*Makes 6 servings.*

# Autumn Chicken Stew

**3 pounds skinless, boneless chicken breasts cut into 2-inch cubes**
**Salt (or salt substitute) and freshly ground pepper to taste**
**Flour for dredging**
**2 tablespoons olive oil**
**1 large yellow onion, diced**
**4 to 5 cloves garlic, minced**
**3 sprigs thyme**
**2 bay leaves**
**2 cups red wine**
**2 cups canned diced tomatoes, with their juices**
**4 cups low-sodium chicken broth**
**4 large carrots, peeled and cut into 1-inch pieces**
**4 large parsnips, peeled and cut into 1-inch pieces**
**2 large russet potatoes, diced**

Season the chicken to taste. Dredge it in flour, shake off the excess, and set aside. Heat the olive oil in a heavy soup pot or Dutch oven over medium-high heat. Sear the meat on all sides; adjust the heat if necessary so that the chicken is well browned, but does not burn. Add the onions, garlic, thyme, and bay leaves and cook 2 minutes before adding the red wine. Use a wooden spoon to scrape any caramelized sediment from the bottom of the pan and cook until the wine is almost completely evaporated.

Next, add the tomatoes with their juices and the chicken broth and bring to a boil. Reduce heat to a simmer and cook until the meat is tender, approximately 1 hour.

Add the carrots, parsnips, and potatoes and cook until the vegetables are completely tender, approximately 20 additional minutes. (The potatoes serve as a thickener.) Adjust the seasoning to taste, remove the bay leaves, and serve in a deep tureen. Add a salad and hearty whole wheat or brown bread, if you like.

*Makes 8 servings.*

**While root vegetables were quite common in our grandmother's kitchen, today they are often overlooked. Less popular than other vegetables, root vegetables such as beets, carrots, rutabagas, turnips, parsnips, onions, garlic, daikon, and ginger are packed with nutrition, flavor, and cancer-fighting nutrients. When they are added to almost any dish, such as soup, stews, and casseroles, they are easiest to sneak into the family meal plan.**

**Economical and plentiful during the fall and winter months, root vegetables are a healthful addition to seasonal soups and stews. When selecting these vegetables look for those that are firm and of medium size. At home store them in a dry and dark place until you are ready to cook them. It is expected that the federal advisory committee will soon increase its daily recommendation for vegetables from five to thirteen servings a day. This increase will require more creative uses for fruits and vegetables in your everyday cooking. For instance, grated carrots add body and nutrients to your spaghetti sauce. And rutabagas may be added to mashed potatoes or stews and casseroles.**

## Winter Chicken

This is a very easy and very tasty recipe. It warms your heart and lifts your spirits on a cold winter day without being too heavy.

**4 boneless skinless chicken breasts**
**3 cloves of garlic, crushed**
**1 large onion, chopped**
**1/2 cup chopped green pepper**
**3 stalks celery, sliced**
**1 quart chicken broth**
**2 cups frozen mixed vegetables**

Combine the above ingredients, except the frozen vegetables, in a large pot and bring to a quick boil, reduce heat to low, and simmer for about an hour or until the meat is fork-tender. Remove meat from pot; and when it is sufficiently cool to handle, dice the meat and return it to the pot. Add mixed vegetables during the last 15 minutes of cooking time. Remove pot top and continue to cook uncovered until the broth cooks down to desired consistency. If you desire thicker gravy, combine 3 tablespoons of flour with 1 cup of water, mix well to remove any lumps, and rapidly stir into your stew while cooking. Serve over rice, if desired, and try substituting brown for white rice. Changing lifetime eating habits is an evolutionary process. If like my husband, you are not quite ready to accept brown rice, try wild rice. Whether you chose white or wild, add chopped steamed vegetables into your rice, gradually using more vegetables and less rice. In this way you add fiber and flavor while hopefully reducing carbs and calories depending on the vegetables used. Add more broth to any that's left over and serve it as soup the next day.

*Makes 4 servings*

# Black Bean Stew

**1 pound black beans**
**10 cups unsalted chicken broth**
**2 green bell peppers, seeded and coarsely chopped**
**2 bay leaves**
**4 slices bacon or 3 tablespoons vegetable oil**
**1 large yellow onion**
**3 cloves garlic, minced**
**1 small pumpkin (2 to 3 pounds), peeled and seeded**
**1 teaspoon ground cumin**
**Pinch cayenne pepper**
**1 teaspoon salt or to taste**
**Black pepper to taste**
**3 to 4 cups cooked white rice (may substitute brown or wild rice)**
**1/4 cup sherry**
**Hot pepper sauce**

Pick over beans to remove foreign objects and soak overnight in sufficient cold water to cover beans by 2 inches. Drain and rinse beans before cooking. Drain beans, then put about 10 cups of broth in a large pot. Add the beans, half of the green pepper, and the bay leaves to the pot; bring to a rapid boil, reduce the heat to low, and simmer for 1 hour. Remove bay leaves. Cut pumpkin into 1/2- to 1-inch cubes and set aside. Add pepper, onion, garlic, pumpkin, cumin, cayenne pepper, salt, and pepper to the skillet after removing bacon. Cook vegetables about 15 minutes over medium-high heat, or until softened. Add vegetables to beans and cook another hour, uncovered, or until beans are tender. In a separate skillet cook the bacon crisp and remove it to a paper towel to drain. Set the bacon aside for a later use.

Stir in sherry just prior to serving. Serve over rice and garnish with crumbled bacon for a complete meal. Allow each guest to season individual servings with hot pepper sauce to taste.

*Makes 6 to 8 servings.*

# Southern Butter Beans & Chicken

**2 cups all purpose flour**
**1 tablespoon salt**
**1 tablespoon freshly ground black pepper**
**1 teaspoon paprika**
**1/2 teaspoon onion powder**
**1 3-pound fryer, cut up**
**Vegetable oil**
**1 1/4 cups chopped onion**
**1/2 cup chopped green pepper**
**1 1/2 cups chicken broth**
**3 cups fresh butter beans (frozen may be substituted)**

Combine the flour and next four seasoning ingredients in a zip top storage bag, seal the top, and shake to blend. Next, wash the chicken pieces under cold running water, drain, and pat dry. Add the chicken, a few pieces at a time, to the plastic storage bag containing the flour and shake to coat. Repeat until all chicken has been coated with flour. Allow the bag to sit for a few minutes before shaking the chicken a second time to coat well. Remove the chicken from the bag, shaking excess flour back into the bag. Add additional flour mixture to the bag as needed. Next, on a medium-high burner, heat approximately 1/4-inch of the oil in a large pot. Lightly brown chicken on all sides, reduce heat to medium, and continue frying, turning regularly, for an additional 10 minutes. Remove chicken from the pot and place on a paper towel–lined plate. Remove all but 3 tablespoons of the vegetable oil from the pot. Sauté onion and bell pepper until the onion is transparent. Add 2 tablespoons of flour from the plastic bag, using additional flour as needed, and sauté, stirring constantly, for approximately 3 minutes. Add chicken broth and butter beans, return chicken to the pot, reduce to a simmer, and cook an additional 35 to 40 minutes, or until the beans are tender and the chickens juices run clear when pierced with a fork.

*Makes 4 to 6 servings.*

## Mustard Greens with Smoked Turkey

**4 bunches of mustard greens**
**2 quarts low-sodium chicken broth**
**1 cup chopped onion**
**1 garlic clove, minced**
**1 tablespoon seasoned salt (or to taste)**
**1/2 teaspoon ground red pepper**
**5 thyme sprigs**
**1 bay leaf**
**3 8-ounce smoked turkey wing drumettes, skinned**

Trim thick stems from mustard greens and discard. Coarsely chop leaves. Combine greens, broth, and remaining ingredients in a large stockpot; bring to a boil. Cover, reduce heat, and simmer 45 minutes or until tender. Remove thyme sprigs, turkey wings, and bay leaf.

Place broth and skinned turkey wing drumettes in a large pot and bring to a rapid boil. Reduce heat to low and simmer for 30 minutes. While the turkey is boiling, prepare the turnip greens by removing thick stalks and discarding any yellowed or badly blemished leaves. Wash greens under cold running water and rinse any remaining sand from the sink. Fill sink with cold water, add greens, and plunge up and down several times to wash any remaining sand and sediment from the greens. Several washings may be needed, but are not usually necessary with store-bought greens. Roll leaves cigar fashion and slice into horizontal segments slightly smaller than 1/4 inch.

Next, gradually stir in the greens, allowing each batch to wilt before adding more greens and remaining ingredients. Bury the smoked turkey in the simmering greens. Cover and reduce the heat to medium-low. Continue cooking the greens an additional 30 minutes. Uncover the pot and cook an additional 15 minutes, or until the greens are tender to personal taste, stirring occasionally.

*Makes 8 servings.*

---

**One thing that I have learned is to occasionally and very judiciously indulge my food cravings. Over time I found that if I ignored them, I ate all of the good foods and nibbled around the bad food until I finally gave in and overindulged in whatever it was that I was originally craving. So now I try to eat less of what it is that I really want from the very beginning. I prefer this more balanced approach, which some call a "lifestyle choice." I prefer "lifestyle adjustment," which allows me to *readjust* as necessary, and I never feel deprived. It's not a diet, so I never have the guilt associated with "cheating." As a result, I still enjoy fried fish and chicken on special occasions; however, I now try to plan for these indulgences. I have included some of my favorite recipes for those of you who, like me, occasionally indulge.**

---

# Fried Chicken & Waffles

What do Roscoe's of Hollywood and Gladys Knight and Ron Winans' Chicken and Waffles, Atlanta, have in common? Why chicken and waffles, of course. While this delicious dish has migrated to the West Coast, its roots remain firmly planted in the South.

## FRIED CHICKEN

My friend Cassandra Bethels's delicious recipe for fried chicken appeared in my first cookbook, *The African American Heritage Cookbook*. It is still one of my favorite ways to prepare fried chicken.

**1 2½- to 3-pound fryer, cut up**
**2 teaspoons onion powder**
**1½ teaspoons garlic powder**
**1½ teaspoons pepper**
**2 teaspoons seasoned salt**
**2 large onions, sliced thin**
**Solid shortening**
**¼ cup butter**
**Flour**

Wash chicken, pat dry, and set aside. Mix together the next 4 seasoning ingredients and use to season chicken. In a large non-reactive bowl, thoroughly combine the chicken and the sliced onions. Cover tightly and (this is the important part) refrigerate overnight. In a large, heavy skillet heat three inches of shortening to approximately 375°F. Add butter to the shortening. Discard onions and coat the chicken with flour, shaking off the excess, and place the chicken in hot oil. Do not crowd the pan. Cook on each side for approximately 15 minutes or until golden. Repeat as necessary. Test doneness by piercing the thickest part of the chicken with a fork. When done, the juices should run clear.

### WAFFLES

**2 cups all-purpose flour**
**1 teaspoon baking powder**
**1/2 teaspoon salt**
**1/2 cup sugar**
**1/8 teaspoon nutmeg**
**2 eggs (at room temperature) separated (reserve the whites)**
**2 cups cold milk**
**1/4 cup butter, melted**

Place the dry ingredients in a large bowl and mix to combine. In a separate bowl, combine the egg yolks, milk and butter. Add to the flour mixture and stir until just moistened. Beat egg whites until stiff peaks form and gently fold into the batter. Bake, according to manufacturer's directions, in an oiled, preheated waffle iron. Separate into 16-inch squares. Serve with butter and cane or maple syrup.

*Makes 8 servings.*

## Sunday Fried Chicken & Homemade Buttermilk Biscuits

This chicken is so good and crispy that you won't want to wait until Sunday! Enjoy.

**2 3- to 4-pound fryers, cut up**
**1 1/2 cups all-purpose flour**
**1/2 cup cornmeal**
**1/4 cup cornstarch**
**1 tablespoon salt**
**1 teaspoon pepper**
**2 1/4 teaspoons paprika**
**1/8 teaspoon cayenne pepper**
**3/4 teaspoon dried oregano**

**1/2 teaspoon onion powder**
**1 teaspoon rubbed sage**
**1 teaspoon black pepper**
**2 eggs, well beaten**
**1/4 cup water**
**Vegetable oil**

Wash fryer pieces well under warm running water and place in a colander to drain. In a large zip top plastic storage bag add the dry ingredients, shake well to combine, and set aside. Combine egg and water in a shallow dish and mix well. Dip chicken in egg mixture, one piece at a time; place in bag a few pieces at a time and shake to coat. In a cast iron skillet heat 1 inch of oil to 375°F. Add chicken and fry for 3 to 5 minutes on each side or until crispy and golden brown. Place chicken in two ungreased 15-inch × 10-inch × 1-inch baking pans. Bake uncovered at 350 degrees for 25 to 30 minutes or until, when pierced with a fork, the chicken's juices run clear.

*Makes 18 pieces.*

### HOMEMADE BUTTERMILK BISCUITS

**2 cups all-purpose flour**
**2 teaspoons baking powder**
**1/2 teaspoon baking soda**
**1/2 teaspoon salt**
**1/2 cup solid shortening**
**3/4 cup buttermilk**

Preheat oven to 450°F. In a large bowl, combine the first four ingredients. Using a fork or pastry blender, cut in shortening until the mixture resembles coarse cornmeal. Blend in the buttermilk until a soft dough is formed. Turn out onto a lightly floured surface and knead lightly for 7 to 8 minutes. Roll to 1/2-inch thickness and cut out with a floured biscuit cutter. Reroll scraps and cut until all dough is used. Place biscuits on an ungreased cookie sheet, approximately 1 inch apart, and bake until golden, approximately 15 minutes. For a delicious treat, serve these biscuits hot with either homemade fig preserves (see recipe below) or strawberry jam.

*Makes approximately 18 to 24 biscuits.*

### FIG PRESERVES

**6 quarts figs**
**1 cup baking soda**
**6 quarts water**
**4 pounds sugar**
**3 quarts water**

Spread figs on the bottom of a well scrubbed sink and sprinkle with baking soda. Pour 6 quarts of boiling water over the figs and allow them to stand undisturbed for 5 to 7 minutes. Drain the water away from the figs, rinse, and fill sink with cold water. Wash figs in this cold water bath, drain, and repeat.

Next, combine the sugar and 3 quarts of hot water in a large pot to make a syrup. Add the figs to the syrup mixture and bring to a rapid boil, cooking until the figs become transparent and tender. Remove the figs from the syrup and set aside. Continue to cook and boil down the syrup until it thickens to the consistency of maple syrup. Pour syrup over figs, ensuring the figs are completely covered. Allow figs to stand overnight before packing the figs into canning jars and covering with syrup. Process in a water bath canner at 212°F for 25 minutes or according to manufacturer's directions.

*Makes 8 quarts.*

---

## Spicy Fried Chicken with Spicy Tomato Salad

This is an adaptation of Caribbean fried chicken. If you like spicy, you will love this chicken.

**1 4-pound chicken, cut up**
**2 medium-size onions, finely chopped**
**1 tablespoon parsley, finely minced**
**1½ tablespoons fresh thyme, finely chopped**

**1 tablespoon fresh marjoram, minced**
**1/2 teaspoon ground cloves**
**1/4 teaspoon ground ginger**
**3 garlic cloves, minced**
**2 jalapeño chili peppers, seeded and chopped**
**1 teaspoon paprika**
**Juice of 1 lime**
**Salt to taste**
**2 cups all-purpose flour**
**1 tablespoon salt**
**1 tablespoon freshly ground black pepper**
**2 eggs, lightly beaten**
**Peanut or canola oil for frying**

Combine the chicken with the next 11 ingredients and refrigerate for 2 to 3 hours. Combine the flour, salt, and pepper, mix well and set aside. Place approximately 1 cup of the flour mixture into a paper or plastic bag and add the chicken, a few pieces at a time, to the bag and shake to coat. Allow the bag to sit for a few minutes before shaking the chicken a second time to coat well. Remove the chicken from the bag, shaking excess flour back into the bag. Add additional flour mixture to the bag as needed. Dip chicken in beaten egg and return to flour mixture to recoat. Next, on a medium-high burner, heat approximately 1/4-inch of the oil in a large skillet. Lightly brown chicken on all sides, reduce heat to medium, and continue frying, turning regularly, until chicken is cooked through. When a fork is inserted into the thickest part of the meat, the juices should run clear. Drain well on paper towels, and serve hot. Seal any unused flour mixture in a plastic bag and refrigerate or freeze for future use. To bake follow the steps up to frying and then place the chicken in a preheated 350° oven and bake for 40 to 50 minutes or until cooked through. The chicken is done when a piece is pierced at its thickest part and the juice runs clear.

*Makes 4 servings.*

### SPICY TOMATO SALAD

**12 plum tomatoes**
**1 teaspoon caster sugar**
**Ground black pepper to taste**
**1 medium-size Bermuda onion, peeled and sliced**
**1 red chili pepper, finely sliced**
**1/4 cup lime juice**
**1/4 cup extra-virgin olive oil**
**1 teaspoon fresh gingerroot, peeled and grated**
**2 teaspoons light soy sauce**
**2 teaspoons chopped coriander leaves**
**3 green onions, thinly sliced**

Slice the tomatoes and gently toss in a bowl with the sugar and pepper. In a separate bowl, mix together the onion, chili, lime juice, olive oil, and grated ginger. Allow tomatoes to stand undisturbed for 15 minutes before combining them with the lime mixture. Add the soy sauce, coriander and green onion. Chill well before serving with the spicy fried chicken.

*Makes 6 to 8 servings.*

# Buttermilk Fried Chicken & Hot Biscuits with Fried Apples

**2 cups buttermilk**
**1 tablespoon curry powder**
**1 tablespoon kosher salt, divided**
**2 teaspoons ground black pepper**
**1 3-pound fryer, cut up**
**1 1/2 cups all-purpose flour**
**2 teaspoons chili powder**
**1/2 teaspoon paprika**
**1/4 teaspoon onion powder**
**Vegetable oil**

In a large bowl, combine the buttermilk and curry powder. In a separate bowl, combine the salt and pepper and mix well to blend. Measure three teaspoons of the salt and pepper mixture into the buttermilk. Mix well. Add the chicken and turn to coat. Cover and refrigerate overnight. The next day, combine the flour, 1 teaspoon of the salt and pepper mixture, chili powder, paprika, and onion powder in a shallow dish. Mix well to blend. Remove the chicken from the buttermilk, allowing excess to drip back into the bowl. Dip chicken in the flour mixture and turn to coat, shake excess flour from chicken, and place on a foil-lined baking sheet. Refrigerate 20 minutes. Pour vegetable oil in a cast iron skillet to a depth of 1/2 inch. Heat oil over medium-high heat to 375°F. Place chicken in the hot oil, skin side down, and reduce heat to medium-low. Cover the pan with a lid and cook until brown, approximately 12 minutes. Turn chicken over and cook uncovered until the chicken is golden brown and cooked through so that when it is pierced with a fork, the juices run clear.

*Makes 4 to 6 servings.*

# Homemade Buttermilk Biscuits

There is no taste treat better than hot from the oven homemade buttermilk biscuits on a cold winter morning. Just thinking about them, I can almost smell their fragrance and taste the delicious strawberry preserves that my mother served with them. So here's another version to try.

**3 cups all purpose flour**
**3 teaspoons baking powder**
**3/4 teaspoon baking soda**
**1 teaspoon salt**
**3/4 cup Crisco shortening, well chilled**
**3/4 cup buttermilk**

Preheat oven to 425°F. In a large bowl, sift together flour, baking powder, baking soda, and salt. Cut shortening into the flour mixture with a pastry blender until the mixture forms coarse crumbs. Add buttermilk, tossing with a fork, until dough holds together and lightly knead, just a few times, until smooth. Next, turn the dough onto a floured surface and form into a 3/4-inch-thick disk. Then using a biscuit cutter or glass dipped in flour, cut out biscuits and place them approximately 2 inches apart on an ungreased baking sheet. Reform any leftover dough and repeat the process. Place in the preheated oven and bake for about 12 to 15 minutes, until golden brown. Serve piping hot with butter and fried apples.

*Makes 12 biscuits.*

### SOUTHERN FRIED APPLES

**1/4 cup butter**
**2 pounds tart unpeeled apples, washed, cored, and quartered**
**1/3 cup sugar**
**2 1/4 teaspoons cinnamon**

Melt butter in a heavy skillet over medium heat. Add apples, cover, and cook over medium heat until soft, approximately 5 to 10 minutes.

Combine sugar and cinnamon, mix to blend. Uncover apples and sprinkle with sugar and cinnamon. Cook until lightly browned on underside.

*Makes 6 to 8 servings.*

## Tasty Fried Chicken & Hot Biscuits with Apple Butter

Chicken and biscuits just like your mother used to make!

**2 cups flour**
**3 tablespoons dry mustard**
**3 tablespoons sweet paprika**
**1 1/2 teaspoons onion powder**
**1/8 teaspoon red pepper**
**1 1/2 tablespoons celery salt**

2 tablespoons fresh ground black pepper
1 tablespoon Lawry's Seasoned Salt
$^1/_4$ teaspoon poultry seasoning
1 teaspoon thyme
1 teaspoon crushed rosemary
1 teaspoon dried oregano, lightly crushed
1 to 2 teaspoons salt, to taste (optional)
$3^1/_2$- to $4^1/_2$- pound broiler-fryer chicken, cut up, washed, and dried
Peanut oil or canola oil, for pan frying

Combine the flour and seasoning ingredients, mix well. Place approximately 1 cup of the flour mixture into a paper or plastic bag and add the chicken, a few pieces at a time, to the bag and shake to coat. Add additional flour mixture to the bag as needed. Allow the bag to sit for a few minutes before shaking the chicken a second time to coat well. Remove the chicken from the bag, shaking excess flour back into the bag. Next, on a medium-high burner, heat approximately $^1/_4$ inch of the oil in a large skillet. Lightly brown chicken on all sides, reduce heat to medium, and continue frying, turning regularly, until chicken is cooked through. When a fork is inserted into the thickest part of the meat, the juices should run clear. Drain well on paper towels, and serve hot. Seal any unused flour mixture in a plastic bag and refrigerate or freeze for future use. Serve with hot biscuits and apple butter just like Mom used to do on cold winter afternoons. Apple butter is available in most grocery stores, but why not make your own, just like mom's! For delicious biscuits, see recipe on page 196.

*Makes 6 to 8 servings.*

## APPLE BUTTER

8 pounds ripe apples (Jonathan, Winesap, or other flavorful apple)
4 cups sweet cider
3 cups firmly packed dark brown sugar
1 teaspoon ground cloves
$2^1/_4$ teaspoons ground cinnamon
$^1/_4$ teaspoon ground allspice
Zest of 1 lemon

Wash the apples. Remove their stems, core and peel, and quarter them. In a large pot, over medium heat, cook the apples in the cider until they are soft. Remove the pot from the heat and allow mixture to cool before pressing the apples into a puree. To each cup of puree, add ½ cup sugar at a time, up to three cups, depending on taste. Add the spices and lemon zest. Return the fruit to the pot and continue to cook over low heat, stirring constantly, until the sugar is dissolved and the mixture thickens. Test doneness by placing a small amount of the mixture on a cold saucer. The outside surface of the portion tested should show a light sheen upon standing. When no rim of liquid separates from around the edge of the butter, it is done. Pour into sterilized jars and seal according to the manufacturer's directions.

*Makes 3 to 4 pints.*

# Fried Catfish & Hushpuppies

## JIMMY STINSON'S CATFISH

The succulent sweet and mild flavor of today's farm-raised catfish is perfectly showcased by the ingredients in this recipe. One of my favorites, it first appeared in *The African-American Heritage Cookbook*.

**2 pounds whole catfish**
**4 cups Louisiana hot sauce**
**2 cups yellow cornmeal**
**2 cups all-purpose flour**
**1 cup blackened catfish seasoning**
**2 tablespoons salt**
**¼ cup black pepper**

Marinate catfish in hot sauce for 2 hours. Meanwhile, mix the meal, flour, and spices together and use it to coat the fish. Heat shortening to approximately 350 degrees F., and fry fish until golden brown. You may have to lower temperature if fish is frying too fast.

*Makes 4 servings.*

### HUSHPUPPIES

**2 1/2 cups self-rising white cornmeal**
**1/3 cup chopped green pepper**
**1/4 cup chopped onion**
**1 teaspoon salt**
**1 teaspoon sugar**
**1/4 teaspoon nutmeg**
**1/4 teaspoon ground cayenne pepper**
**1/2 teaspoon ground black pepper**
**1 cup buttermilk**
**2 large eggs**
**Vegetable oil**

Combine the first eight ingredients in a large mixing bowl and mix well to blend. Form a well in the center of the cornmeal mixture and set aside. In a separate bowl combine the buttermilk and eggs, mix well and pour into the well of the cornmeal mixture, stirring until just blended. Allow the mixture to stand at room temperature for 30 minutes. Pour oil in a Dutch oven or cast-iron skillet to a depth of 2 inches. Heat the oil to 375°F and drop the cornmeal batter by heaping teaspoonfuls into the hot oil. Fry in batches for 2 to 3 minutes on each side or until golden. Drain on brown paper bags or paper towels and pile onto a plate with fried catfish. Serve family-style with cole slaw and lots of family fun and laughter.

*Makes 18 to 24 hushpuppies, depending on size.*

## Fried Catfish & Cheesy Grits

**6 4- to 6-ounce catfish filets**
**2 cups buttermilk**
**2 cups yellow cornmeal**
**1/4 cup flour**
**1 tablespoon seasoned salt**
**2 teaspoons pepper**

**3/4 teaspoon onion powder**
**1/2 teaspoon garlic powder**
**Salt and pepper to taste**
**Vegetable oil**

Place catfish filets in a single layer in a shallow dish; cover with the buttermilk and chill for 1 hour. While the fish are chilling, combine the cornmeal and the next 5 ingredients in a shallow dish. Remove the filets from the refrigerator and allow them to stand at room temperature for 10 minutes before removing them from the buttermilk. Allow the excess buttermilk to drip off the fish back into the bowl. Season fillets with salt and pepper to taste and dredge in flour. Fry in oil that has been poured to a depth of 1 1/2 inches and heated to 350°F. Cook in batches for about three to four minutes on each side or until golden brown. Drain on brown paper bags or paper towels.

*Makes 3 to 4 servings.*

## CHEESY GRITS

Hominy grits are a Southern institution. The process of making hominy grits begins when corn kernels, dried on the cob, are removed by soaking the cobs in a special solution to soften the kernels. Next, the kernels are hulled and degermed using friction and dried. The coarse whitish grains we enjoy as grits are then ground from hominy.

**4 cups boiling water**
**1 teaspoon salt**
**1 cup hominy grits (do not use instant)**
**1/2 cup butter**
**1 cup grated cheddar cheese**
**2 eggs**
**Up to 1 cup milk**

Preheat oven to 350 degrees. In a large pot, bring water to a rolling boil; add salt and grits. Reduce to a simmer and stir and cook grits for 3 to 4 minutes, or until grits thicken. Remove grits from heat and stir in butter and cheese; mix well. In a large measuring cup combine eggs and sufficient milk to make 1 cup. Add the milk mixture to the grits and mix well to combine. Pour into casserole and bake in the preheated oven for approximately 45 minutes. Cut the grits into squares and serve hot.

*Makes 6 servings.*

## Almost Any Fried Fish with Just Grits

This recipe works equally well with bream, crappie, and the perennially popular catfish.

**3/4 cup yellow cornmeal**
**1/4 cup all-purpose flour**
**2 teaspoons salt**
**1 teaspoon cayenne pepper**
**1 teaspoon paprika**
**1/4 teaspoon garlic powder**
**1/2 teaspoon onion powder**
**1/4 teaspoon salt**
**8 4-ounce catfish fillets**
**Salt and pepper**
**Peanut or canola oil for frying**

Combine first 8 ingredients in a shallow dish. Salt and pepper fish to taste. Dredge fish in cornmeal mixture, coating evenly. Shake off excess cornmeal mixture, place on a plate in a single layer, and refrigerate for 20 minutes before frying. Place approximately 1 1/2 inches oil into a deep cast iron skillet. Heat over a medium to medium-high burner until the oil just begins to smoke. Add fish and fry in batches, 5 to 6 minutes or until golden brown. Adjust heat as necessary to prevent burning. Drain fish on paper towels. Serve piping hot with tartar sauce, hot sauce, or mustard. We eat fish and grits for breakfast most often, but it is served almost as often for dinner. If you drop in for dinner, it's more than likely that you will receive Cheesy Grits (recipe on pages 201–202). If you are serving fried fish with fries or hushpuppies and slaw, don't forget the mustard, hot sauce, or tartar sauce. The recipe for homemade tartar sauce follows.

## JUST GRITS

I know I can share this secret with you, and only you; so, when asked what you put in your grits to make them so flavorful, smile like a Cheshire cat and respond, "Just grits."

**5 cups water**
**1/2 teaspoon salt**
**1 cup hominy grits (do not use instant)**
**2 eggs well beaten**
**2 tablespoons butter**

In a large pan add salt to water, bring to a boil. Stir in hominy grits slowly. Reduce heat and stir until thickened, approximately 5 minutes. Cook for 15 minutes longer, stirring occasionally to keep from sticking. During the last 10 minutes of cooking time, stir rapidly while adding your eggs and butter.

*Makes 8 servings.*

## TARTAR SAUCE

**1 1/4 cups finely chopped onion**
**2 3/4 cups celery, chopped**
**1 cup dill pickle relish**
**1/4 cup sweet pickle relish**
**3 cups mayonnaise**

Drain the juices from the onions, celery, and relish or the onion juice especially will make your tartar sauce bitter. Combine with the mayonnaise and mix well. Refrigerate to chill before serving with your hot fish.

# Shrimp & Grits

A new Southern favorite, this fast flavorful dish will soon become a favorite of your family as well.

**1 medium onion, minced**
**1 green bell pepper, minced**
**3 cloves garlic, minced**
**2 tablespoons vegetable oil**
**1 pound medium-size shrimp, shelled and deveined**
**2 tablespoons Worcestershire sauce**
**1 pinch cayenne pepper**
**2 cups hot cooked grits**
**2 tablespoons softened butter, divided**

Cook onion, pepper, and garlic in oil over moderately low heat, stirring, until onion is translucent and limp. Add shrimp and cook mixture over moderately high heat, stirring, for 3 minutes, or until shrimp are cooked through. Shrimp should be pink and the tails slightly curled. Stir in Worcestershire sauce and cayenne pepper. Spoon hot grits onto platter, top with dots of butter, and arrange the shrimp mixture around and over grits.

*Makes 4 servings.*

# Spicy Shrimp & Rice

**6 tablespoons olive oil, divided**
**1 large onion, finely sliced**
**3 cloves of garlic, finely minced**
**2 very ripe medium tomatoes, peeled**
**2 bay leaves**
**1 teaspoon dried parsley leaves**
**1/4 teaspoon saffron**
**Salt and freshly ground black pepper to taste**
**1/4 teaspoon ground allspice**

**1/8 teaspoon chili powder**
**1 cup long-grain or Basmati rice**
**1 pound medium shrimp, shelled and deveined**
**1 tablespoon minced parsley**

Slowly simmer the onions in 2 tablespoons of the oil until they are golden. Add the garlic, tomatoes, bay leaves, parsley, and saffron. Cover and simmer for 15 minutes.

Next season the dish with salt, pepper, allspice, and chili powder. Boil the rice according to package directions until it is just done. Strain rice into a sieve and keep warm over a pot of boiling water. Add the shrimp to the tomato mixture and cook, covered, over high heat for 3 minutes. Stir in the remaining 4 tablespoons of oil and parsley into the rice. Serve immediately. Arrange the rice in a ring on plates and place the shrimp in the middle.

*Makes 2 to 4 servings.*

# Roast Pork in Peach Sauce

This recipe first appeared in *A Taste of Freedom: A Cookbook with Recipes and Remembrances from The Hampton Institute.* However, the recipe was too delicious not to reintroduce it in this recipe book from Georgia, the Peach State!

**5-pound pork loin roast**
**3 garlic cloves, quartered**
**3 tablespoons vegetable oil**
**1 1/2 teaspoons salt**
**1 teaspoon onion powder**
**1/4 teaspoon ground allspice**
**1/2 teaspoon ground black pepper**
**1/8 teaspoon ground cloves**
**2 medium onions, sliced**
**4 bay leaves**

Wash the pork roast, pat it dry, and pierce it in several places with a two-prong fork. Force a garlic quarter into each hole. If necessary, use a paring knife to widen the hole. Rub the roast with vegetable oil and set aside. Combine the next 5 seasoning ingredients, mix well, and rub into the roast. Refrigerate for 3 hours, or if possible, overnight. Preheat the oven to 325°F. Combine the Spiced Peach Syrup ingredients (see below) and set aside. Place the onions and bay leaves in the bottom of a roasting pan. Place roast on bed of onions, fat side down. Roast the pork loin, allowing 35 minutes' cooking time per pound. Baste occasionally with Spiced Peach Syrup (see Spiced Peach Syrup recipe below). During the last 15 to 20 minutes of cooking time, cover the roast with peaches, attaching them with toothpicks.

*Makes 10–12 servings.*

# Spiced Peach Syrup

**1 large can peach halves in heavy syrup**
**1/2 teaspoon ground allspice**
**1/2 teaspoon ground cinnamon**
**1/8 teaspoon ground cloves**

Combine the peaches and syrup with the remaining ingredients, and use to baste and dress the roast according to the above directions.

*Makes approximately 1/2 cup syrup.*

# Cranberry-Orange Glazed Ham

Ring in the holidays and dazzle your guests with this beautiful ham, which looks absolutely festive on any holiday table!

**1 7- to 8-pound smoked, fully cooked ham half**
**1 cup cranberry concentrate**

**1/2 cup orange juice**
**1/2 cup ginger ale**
**1/2 cup firmly packed brown sugar**
**2 tablespoons vegetable oil**
**1 tablespoon white vinegar**
**2 teaspoons dry mustard**
**1/2 teaspoon ground ginger**
**1/2 teaspoon ground cloves**
**1/8 teaspoon ground nutmeg**
**Orange slices**
**Fresh cranberries**

Trim the skin away from the ham, leaving a quarter inch of fat. Place the ham in a large roasting bag. Combine the remaining ingredients and pour over the ham. Tie the bag tightly, place in large bowl that allows the glaze to form around the ham without being too tight. Refrigerate the ham 8 hours or overnight, turning occasionally. Remove the ham from the bag, reserving the marinade. Preheat the oven to 325°F. Place the ham on a rack in a shallow roasting pan. Insert a meat thermometer into the ham without allowing it to rest on the bone, which could cause a false reading. Baste the ham with the reserved marinade every 15 to 20 minutes. Bake at 325°F for 2 to 2 1/2 hours or until the meat thermometer registers 140 degrees. If you do not have a meat thermometer, bake the ham at 325°F, allowing 18 to 24 cooking minutes per pound. Garnish ham with orange slices held in place with a toothpick. Hide each toothpick by spearing a cranberry on it.

*Makes 12 servings.*

# Southern-Style Barbecued Pork Sandwiches

A delicious recipe that can also be used on your grill or with your smoker!

**6–8 pound Boston butt, trimmed of excess fat to 1/4 inch**
**Mop Sauce (recipe follows)**
**Southern Rub (recipe follows)**

Prepare the Mop Sauce and refrigerate. Combine the Southern Rub ingredients. Using a little more than half of the rub mixture, coat meat on all sides, place the roast in a plastic bag, seal tight, and refrigerate it overnight. The next day, remove the roast from the refrigerator and allow it to rest at room temperature for 45 minutes. Preheat the oven to 350°F, remove the plastic bag, and bake the roast uncovered for 45 minutes. Reduce temperature to 300°F and cook for an additional 6 to 7 hours or until the pork roast is very tender. Mop the pork with the mopping sauce every 1 1/2 to 2 hours. When roast is cooked through and reaches an internal temperature of 180 degrees, remove it from the baking pan, wrap it tightly in aluminum foil, and allow it to rest for at least 30 minutes. Remove the roast from the foil, and roughly chop or "pull" the pork. Add a small amount of your favorite BBQ sauce, mix well, and serve on hamburger buns with coleslaw on the side (some people garnish their sandwiches with the coleslaw) and icy cold beer.

*Makes 8 to 10 servings.*

## MOP SAUCE

**3/4 tablespoon salt**
**3/4 tablespoon dry mustard**
**1/2 tablespoon garlic powder**
**1/2 tablespoon chili powder**
**1/4 tablespoon bay leaf powder**
**3/4 tablespoon paprika**

**1/2 tablespoon hot sauce (or to taste)**
**1 cup Worcestershire sauce**
**1/2 cup apple cider vinegar**
**1 tablespoon liquid smoke**
**4 cups beef broth**
**1/2 cup vegetable oil**

Combine all ingredients and simmer together for about 15 minutes in a large saucepan. Cool slightly and use as a delicious grilling mop for beef or pork.

*Makes approximately 6 cups.*

### SOUTHERN RUB

**2 tablespoons salt**
**2 tablespoons chili powder**
**1/2 tablespoon coarse black pepper**
**1/2 tablespoon garlic powder**
**1 teaspoon cayenne pepper**
**2 teaspoons dry mustard**
**1/4 cup turbinado sugar**

Combine the above ingredients and use as a rub for pork or beef.

*Makes about 1/2 cup.*

## Oven-Roasted Honey Barbecued Chicken

**2 3-pound fryers, cut up**
**3/4 teaspoon salt**
**3/4 teaspoon black pepper**
**1/4 teaspoon cayenne pepper**
**1 3/4 teaspoons paprika**
**2 large onions, chopped**

**2 8-ounce cans tomato sauce**
**1/2 cup cider vinegar**
**1/2 cup + 1 tablespoon honey**
**1/4 cup Worcestershire sauce**

Wash chicken under warm running water, drain, and pat dry. Place chicken skin side down in an ungreased baking dish. Combine salt and pepper and use to season the chicken. Combine the remaining ingredients, mix well, and pour over the chicken. Bake uncovered in preheated oven for 30 minutes. Turn chicken and bake an additional 20 minutes basting occasionally, or until when pierced with a fork, the chicken juices run clear.

*Makes 8 servings.*

**The following recipes are part of our soul food heritage, which should never be forgotten. More than just Southern cooking, soul food was survival food. Slaves would cleverly prepare dishes using the beef, chicken, and pork sections discarded by their masters, and serve them up with ingredients transplanted with them from their homeland, such as yams, goobers, and black-eyed peas, to make a soul-satisfying meal. Following slavery these foods continued to be served in celebrated soul food restaurants such as Paschals in Atlanta, where Dr. Martin Luther King, Jr., and others met during the 50s and early 60s to plan civil rights strategy. Through the generations, soul food has become black America's national dish. As we sit down to break bread at our homecoming tables, it is a communal offering that recognizes our common ancestral roots. However, now, rather than eating it every day, we often choose to serve soul food on special occasions to celebrate our history and heritage.**

# Collard Greens with Smoked Neck Bones

**2 tablespoons bacon drippings or 5 slices of bacon**
**1 large onion, sliced thin**
**2 pounds smoked pork neck bones**
**1 quart water**
**2 beef bouillon cubes**
**1/2 teaspoon salt**
**1 teaspoon black pepper**
**2 teaspoons crushed red pepper**
**1 teaspoon thyme leaves**
**2 bay leaves**
**5 pounds collard greens**

Heat bacon drippings or render fat from bacon over medium-high heat. Once fat has been rendered from bacon, remove and discard or dice and return to the pot when the collard greens are added. Sauté onion in the drippings until they are translucent. Wash neck bones, removing all gritty bone and other residue from the meat. Add the meat, water, and remaining seasoning ingredients. Bring meat to a quick boil, reduce heat, cover, and simmer over low heat for 1 hour.

While neck bones are cooking, prepare the collard greens by removing thick stalks and discarding any yellowed or badly blemished leaves. Wash greens under cold running water and rinse any remaining sand from the sink. Fill sink with cold water, add greens, and plunge up and down several times to wash any remaining sand and sediment from the greens. Several washings may, but are not usually, necessary with store-bought greens. Stack several leaves, roll them cigar fashion and slice into horizontal segments slightly smaller than 1/4 inch.

When the neck bones have simmered for an hour, remove all but one quart of the juice from the pot and reserve. Gradually stir in the greens, allowing each batch to wilt before adding more greens. Bury the neck bones in the simmering greens. Cover and reduce the heat to medium-low. Continue cooking the greens an additional 30 minutes. Uncover the pot and cook an additional 15 to 30 minutes, or until the greens are tender to personal taste, stirring occasionally. Younger greens will require less cooking time; older greens will require more. Add reserved pot juices as necessary to prevent sticking and scorching. Cook until the greens are tender and the meat nearly falls off the bones. Add additional seasoning to taste.

Serve this delicious country dish with hot buttermilk cornbread, fresh field peas if you've got 'em, and some garden fresh tomatoes and cucumbers with a sprinkling of hot pepper vinegar and some salt and pepper. You know what I'm talkin' 'bout! I'm huuunnnngrrrry *now!* What about you?

*Makes 6 to 8 servings.*

## Smoked Turkey Necks & Collard Greens

**1 pound of smoked turkey necks (or whatever parts are available in your part of the woods)**
**1½ quarts water**
**2 chicken bouillon cubes**
**2 or 3 jalapeño peppers (optional)**
**4 large cloves garlic, minced**
**4 pounds of fresh collards**
**1 medium onion, coarsely chopped**
**2 stalks celery, coarsely chopped**
**1 large green pepper, coarsely chopped**
**1 tablespoon sugar**
**1 tablespoon bacon drippings or vegetable oil (optional)**
**Salt and black pepper to taste**

Wash turkey parts and place them in a Dutch oven. Add water, chicken bouillon cubes, jalapeño peppers, and garlic. Replace the cover and bring mixture to a rapid boil. Reduce the heat to low and simmer 30 minutes. While the turkey is boiling, prepare the collard greens by removing thick stalks and discarding any yellowed or badly blemished leaves. Wash greens under cold running water and rinse any remaining sand from the sink. Fill sink with cold water, add greens, and plunge up and down several times to wash any remaining sand and sediment from the greens. Several washings may be, but are not usually necessary with store-bought greens. Roll leaves cigar fashion and slice into horizontal segments slightly smaller than 1/4 inch.

Next, gradually stir in the greens with the turkey, allowing each batch to wilt before adding more greens. Add onion, celery, green pepper, sugar, drippings or oil, and seasonings to the pot. Bury the smoked turkey in the simmering greens. Cover and reduce the heat to medium-low. Continue cooking the greens an additional 30 minutes. Uncover the pot and cook 15 to 30 minutes more, or until the greens are tender to personal taste, stirring occasionally. Younger greens will require less cooking time; older greens will require more. Add additional liquid as necessary to prevent sticking and scorching. Add additional seasoning to taste.

*Makes 6 servings.*

## Pig's Tails & Turnip Greens

**2 to 3 pounds of pig's tails cut into 2-inch pieces**
**3/4 teaspoon salt**
**2 large onions, chopped**
**1 large bell pepper, chopped**
**2 large cloves of garlic, minced**
**1/8 teaspoon red pepper or to taste**
**1/4 cup bacon drippings**

Wash pig's tails by grasping each tail near its base. Next dip a scrub brush in water and scrub the tail vigorously to remove all traces of scum and particles of dirt. Then wash the tails under cold, running water before patting them dry and placing them in a large, heavy pot with sufficient water to cover.

Bring the water to a boil, add the salt, and cook tails for 30 to 45 minutes. While pig's tails are cooking, prepare greens by removing thick stalks and discarding any yellowed or badly blemished leaves. Wash greens under cold running water and rinse any remaining sand from the sink. Fill sink with cold water, add greens, and plunge up and down several times to wash any remaining sand and sediment from the greens. Several washings may be, but are not usually necessary with store-bought greens. Stack several leaves, roll stacked leaves cigar fashion and slice into horizontal segments slightly smaller than 1/4 inch.

Remove and set aside all but one quart of the liquid and add additional liquid as required to yield one liquid quart. Next, gradually stir in the greens, allowing each batch to wilt before adding more greens, the celery, onion, green pepper, sugar, oil and seasonings to the pot. Bury the pigtails in the simmering greens. Cover and reduce the heat to medium-low. Continue cooking the greens an additional 30 minutes. Stir in bacon drippings, uncover the pot and cook an additional 15 to 30 minutes, or until the pig's tails are tender to personal taste or fork tender (approximately 1 hour) and the greens are tender to personal taste, stirring occasionally. Younger greens will require less cooking time; older greens will require more. Add additional liquid as necessary to prevent sticking and scorching. Add additional seasoning to taste. (For pig's tails and cabbage, substitute approximately two large heads of cabbage for the turnip greens and proceed according to instructions.)

*Makes 6 servings.*

# Pig's Tails & Lima Beans

**2 to 3 pounds of pig's tails cut into 2-inch pieces**
**3/4 teaspoon salt**
**2 large onions, chopped**
**1 large bell pepper, chopped**
**2 large cloves of garlic, minced**
**1/8 teaspoon red pepper or to taste**
**1 pound dried lima beans, washed and soaked overnight**
**1/2 teaspoon dry mustard**
**Salt and freshly ground pepper to taste**

Pick over the peas to remove any foreign objects and soak overnight in sufficient water to cover by 2 to 3 inches. The next day, wash each pig tail by grasping it near its base. Next dip a scrub brush in water and scrub the tail vigorously to remove all traces of scum and particles of dirt. Wash the tails under cold, running water before patting them dry and placing them in a large, heavy pot with sufficient water to cover.

Bring the water to a boil, add the salt and cook the pig's tails for 30 to 45 minutes. Skim away any scum during cooking. Add lima beans and all remaining ingredients. Cook for another 1 to 1½ hours until tender. Add additional water as necessary to prevent the beans from scorching.

*Makes 8 servings.*

# "Chitlins" & Hog Maws

The hog maws (stomach) are added to stretch the more expensive chitterlings (intestines) in this recipe. However, you may substitute chitterlings for the maws if you prefer and disregard the directions for cooking and cleaning maws.

Twenty to 30 pounds of "chitlins," or "chits," if you are in a hurry or feeling particularly refined, is a good start in my family, with the exception of my husband who refrains from the enjoyment of this Southern delicacy. Classified as American soul food, and once prepared by slaves as survival food, they are eaten in many other parts of the world, including Great Britain and even China, as my daughter and I discovered while wandering through L.A.'s China Town. You know we tried them. They were fried with Chinese seasonings and tasted delicious.

**10 pounds of pork hog maws**
**10 pounds pork chitterlings**
**6 quarts water**
**1 tablespoon salt**

**1/2 teaspoon red pepper or to taste**
**2 large yellow onions, quartered**
**2 large green peppers, seeded, quartered, and cut up**
**3 cloves sliced garlic**
**1 large white potato, peeled**
**1/2 lemon, seeded and quartered**
**5 whole cloves**
**3 bay leaves**
**3/4 cup of fresh lemon juice, divided**

**Cleaning Hog Maws:** First, thaw the maws, if frozen. Under running water, remove the fat and debris from maws. Cut maws into 2-inch pieces. Rinse in fresh water several times and set aside.

**Cleaning Chitterlings:** If frozen, thaw chitterlings overnight. Reserve the bucket for collecting and disposing of the debris. Hold a piece of the chitterling in one hand so that the smooth side faces away from you and the fatty membranous lining is clearly visible to you. Take the other hand, or use a knife as my mother did, to remove the three Fs: fat, feed, and feces from the lining. (Oh hush! You sausage eaters partake of chitterling too, as they are still sometimes used as sausage casings.) Proceed carefully, segment by segment, rinse and repeat. When performed correctly, it's a time-consuming task. (I don't eat everyone's chitterlings.) Even pre-cleaned chitterlings should be cleaned again, whether they need it or not. Place waste in the bucket and the cleaned chitterling in a sink full of cold water. After all of the chitterlings have been cleaned in this manner, plunge the chitterlings up and down a few times, drain water from the sink, rinse in this manner several times. Next remove the chitterlings a segment at a time. Wash each segment under cold running water while checking again for the three Fs. Using kitchen shears, cut them in two-inch slices right into a large non-reactive bucket or pot to which a half-cup of lemon juice and two quarts of cold water has been added. (Or as my mother used to do, you can cook them first and cut them up using a large cooking fork to hold them in place and a large knife to cut them.) After all of the chitterlings have been rinsed in this manner, add sufficient water to cover them and allow them to set for two hours before cooking.

**Cooking:** The hog maws are the thickest and must be cooked first. Place the maws in a large pot with three quarts of water. Take into consideration the 10 pounds of chitterlings, which must be added, and use two pots if necessary. Add the onion, green pepper, and salt. Bring the mixture to a boil and allow the maws to cook for an hour and twenty minutes before adding the chitterlings and remaining ingredients. Cover and simmer 4 to 5 hours or until chitterlings are tender. Watch carefully and add additional water as necessary to prevent burning. Remove the top during the last 30 minutes of cooking to allow the juices to cook down and form gravy. Continue to watch closely and add additional water, if required, to prevent scorching. Stir occasionally. Remove and discard the bay leaf, using a fork or spoon. If desired mash the potato against the side of the pot and stir to further thicken the gravy or remove and discard.

As you can see, cleaning chitterlings is a time-consuming process. As in days of old we most often eat them around Thanksgiving and Christmas. My sister-in-law, Erie, has huge family dinners in Chicago and she begins cleaning, cooking, and freezing her chitterlings months ahead of time!

My parents owned a soul food restaurant in Plattsburgh, New York, called "The House by the Side of the Road." Almost every Sunday, I sat in the dining-room with my brother, listening to the band's "Jam Session" while eating chitlins over rice, with a side of collard greens, a mound of my mom's homemade potato salad, a slab of cornbread and some red (cherry) Kool-Aid or sweet tea.

In the summer, if they were barbecuing on the open pit which stood in a screened building on the side of the road, you could add a barbecued rib or two to that meal. As the band's singer crooned the Impressions' "It's All Right," all I could do was lick my fingers and nod my head in agreement.

*Makes 10 to 12 servings (depending on the appetites of your guests).*

# Fried Chitterlings & Hog Maws

**10 pounds of pork hog maws**
**10 pounds pork chitterlings**
**6 quarts water**
**1 tablespoon salt**
**1/2 teaspoon red pepper or to taste**
**1/4 stick of butter**

Clean and cut up the maws and chitterlings according to the directions on page 216. The hog maws are the thickest and must be cooked first. Place the maws in a large pot with three quarts of water. Consider the 10 pounds of chitterlings, which must be added, and use two pots if necessary. Add the onion, green pepper and salt. Bring the mixture to a boil and allow the maws to cook for an hour and twenty minutes before adding the chitterlings and remaining ingredients. Cover and simmer an additional hour and twenty minutes or until chitterlings are tender. Watch carefully and add additional water as necessary to prevent burning.

Drain hog maws and chitterlings from the pot and discard the liquid and onions. Place 1/4 stick of butter in a large skillet and melt over medium high heat. Stir in maws and chitterlings in small batches and stir until lightly browned. Remove to a paper-towel lined plate to drain and repeat the process until all are cooked. Reheat and serve hot with plenty of hot sauce or a jalapeño pepper on the side.

*Makes 8 to 10 servings.*

# Pig's Feet in Spicy Tomato Sauce

**6 medium pig's feet, split, cleaned, and rinsed**
**6 quarts of water**
**2 teaspoons salt**
**3 large onions, coarsely chopped**
**3 large cloves of garlic, minced**

**2 large green peppers, stemmed, seeded, and chopped**
**3 stalks of celery, finely chopped**
**2 jalapeño peppers, seeded and chopped (optional)**
**1/2 cup vinegar**
**1/4 teaspoon ground allspice**
**1/4 teaspoon ground cloves**
**1/4 teaspoon ground nutmeg**
**5 bay leaves**
**3 12-ounce cans tomato sauce**
**1/2 teaspoon sugar**

Wash pig's feet under cold running water. In a large pot (eight quarts or more) bring six quarts of water and salt to a rapid boil. Add pig's feet, onions, garlic, green peppers, and celery to the boiling water; reduce heat and gently simmer for 1 hour. Add the remaining ingredients and simmer an additional two to three hours or until the pig's feet are fork-tender, the meat falls readily from the bones, and the succulent sauce thickens.

# Chicken Feet Stew

My mother, in sharing stories of her childhood, often told me that on Sundays when the preacher came to dinner the best part of the chicken went to him, followed by her father. It was then apportioned according to age, with the youngest children receiving the disappointing feet. I am sure that with so many preachers living in Atlanta during the time period of this book, someone can relate to my mom's story.

**2 pounds skinned chicken feet**
**3 cubes chicken bouillon cubes**
**10 new potatoes halved**
**4 onions, quartered**
**1 1/2 cups baby carrots**
**1 cup green beans, slice into 1-inch sections**
**3 bay leaves**

**4 cloves of garlic, minced**
**Salt and pepper to taste**

If the tough outer skin of the chicken has not been removed, first loosen the skin by passing it through a flame until the skin is blistered all over. Next, use a paper towel to pull off the pieces of parched skin and then discard them. Remove the nail from the base of each toe with kitchen shears or a sharp, heavy knife. Wash the feet and then place them in a stockpot with sufficient water to cover, bring to a boil and cook for 1/2 hour, skimming any sediment from the top as it cooks.

Add bullion cubes, potatoes, onions, carrots, green beans, bay leaves, garlic, salt, and pepper to taste. Simmer until tender, approximately an additional 30 to 45 minutes. Remove bay leaves before serving. The chicken broth can be thickened by combining 2 tablespoons of flour with 1/4 cup of cold water. Mix thoroughly to remove any lumps and drizzle into the simmering mixture while constantly stirring. Add additional salt and pepper to taste and serve hot.

*Makes 6 to 8 servings.*

# Baked Turkey Legs

When chicken feet just won't do, try these meaty turkey legs. If you know your day at home will be busy and you don't have the time or inclination to stand over a hot stove, pop these into the oven and by dinnertime your neighbors will be knocking at your door in hopes of receiving a dinner invitation.

**4 turkey legs**
**Seasoned salt and pepper to taste**
**4 cloves of garlic, crushed**
**1 bell pepper, seeded and coarsely chopped**
**1 onion, coarsely chopped**

Preheat oven to 250°F. Wash turkey legs under cold running water, place in baking dish and season according to taste. Add remaining ingredients and seal tightly with aluminum foil. Place in a preheated oven and allow to cook 4 hours or until meat falls easily from the bones. Remove bones and discard. Serve with rice, mashed potatoes, or a mixture of broccoli, cauliflower, and carrots. If you desire thicker gravy, pour pan drippings into a saucepan. Combine 3 tablespoons of flour with 1 cup of water, mix well to remove any lumps, and rapidly stir into your pan drippings while stirring. Serve over rice, if desired, or with a salad and hearty homemade bread. You choose!

*Makes 4 large servings or 6 small servings.*

**African-American culture and heritage is the blending of many cultures, including Caribbean. It stands to reason that Caribbeans of African descent would be attracted to Atlanta as a major center of black culture. They studied and taught at the AUC and owned businesses on Auburn Street. They also brought their food with them. With its common root in Africa, it's not surprising that it soon found its way to African-American tables. The Caribbean food influence remains strong in Atlanta. Its presence is strongly felt to this day with the plethora of Caribbean restaurants that surround the AUC campus. At lunchtime there is usually a long line. With these recipes, there is no wait.**

# Roast Turkey with Jerk Seasoning

1 12½-pound turkey
¼ cup jerk seasoning spices (see recipe on page 15)
½ cup honey
3 tablespoons lime juice
¼ cup soy sauce (low sodium may be substituted)
3 cups chicken broth (low sodium is acceptable)
Vegetable oil

Remove neck and giblets from the turkey, rinse under cold running water, and pat dry. Use fingers to carefully loosen skin over breast and tops of legs without tearing the skin. Combine jerk spices, honey, lime juice, and soy sauce and rub this mixture onto the turkey. Refrigerate to marinate overnight.

Prepare stuffing (recipe follows) and allow it to cool completely before filling the turkey cavity just before roasting. Place turkey in roasting pan and add chicken broth. Brush top evenly with vegetable oil and bake at 350° F for 30 minutes, then reduce temperature to 325°F for $3^{1}/_{2}$ hours. After one hour, cover turkey with foil to prevent skin from burning. The turkey is ready when it is golden brown and the juice runs clear when pierced in the drumstick joint with a fork. This is also delicious when served with spicy sausage stuffing and Jamaican rice and peas. See recipe below.

*Makes 12 to 15 servings.*

# Spicy Sausage Stuffing

**$3^{1}/_{2}$ pounds lean ground pork (not sausage)**
**3 cloves garlic, minced**
**$^{1}/_{4}$ cup minced parsley**
**1 teaspoon salt**
**1 teaspoon hot pepper sauce**
**$^{1}/_{4}$ teaspoon nutmeg**
**1 teaspoon black pepper**
**$1^{1}/_{4}$ teaspoons thyme**
**1 tablespoon rum**

Combine the above ingredients, blend well, and fill the neck and cavity of the turkey. Skewer cavity closed and bake according to the above directions.

*Makes 6 servings.*

# Jamaican Rice and Peas

**1 cup dried kidney beans, rinsed**
**Approximately 5 cups water, divided**
**1 13½-ounce can coconut milk**
**5 green onions, finely chopped**
**1 jalapeño pepper, seeded and chopped fine**
**3 cloves garlic, peeled and minced**
**2 teaspoons dried thyme**
**2 cups long-grain white rice**
**1½ teaspoons salt**
**½ teaspoon black pepper**

Place the beans and 4 cups cold water in a 4-quart pot. Cover, bring to a boil, remove from the heat, and allow to stand for 1 hour. Drain, and return the beans to the pot. Add the coconut milk, onion, jalapeño pepper, garlic, thyme, and 1 cup cold water. Cover and simmer for 30 minutes until the beans are just tender. Drain the beans, reserving the liquid, return them to the pot, and add the rice, salt, and pepper; measure the reserved liquid and add enough cold water to make 4 cups total. Add the liquid to the pot. Cover, bring to a boil, and reduce the heat to low. Simmer for 15 minutes until the liquid is absorbed. Add more salt and pepper if desired.

*Makes 8 to 10 servings.*

# Oxtail Stew with Saffron Rice

**3 pounds of oxtails, trimmed of excess fat and washed**
**Salt and black pepper**
**2 medium onions, sliced thin**
**¼ cup flour**
**½ teaspoon salt**
**½ teaspoon black pepper**
**⅓ cup vegetable oil**

**2 tomatoes, coarsely chopped**
**1 Scotch bonnet pepper, chopped**
**4 garlic cloves, minced**
**1 large green pepper, seeded and coarsely chopped**
**6 cups hot beef broth**
**3 tablespoons tomato purée**
**1/2 teaspoon dried thyme**
**Salt and black pepper to taste**

Place oxtails in a large bowl and season to taste with salt and black pepper. Add approximately half the onions, garlic, and Scotch bonnet pepper, refrigerate for at least 2 hours or overnight. Combine flour, salt, and black pepper in a bowl and dredge the oxtail pieces in flour mixture, making sure all sides are well covered.

Heat oil over medium-high heat and lightly brown the oxtails. Remove meat from pan, drain off all but 1 to 2 tablespoons of the oil. Add remaining onion, tomato, green pepper, Scotch bonnet, and garlic to pan and sauté lightly. Add hot broth and tomato purée, stir well. Place in an ovenproof dish with meat and thyme, and cook in a medium oven until tender, about 1 1/2 hours. Serve with saffron rice (recipe follows).

*Makes 4 servings.*

## SAFFRON RICE

**1 clove garlic**
**1/4 cup diced onion**
**1/4 cup diced green bell pepper**
**1 diced pimento**
**3 tablespoons olive oil**
**1/4 teaspoon salt (optional)**
**Pinch of fresh ground black pepper**
**Pinch of turmeric**
**1/4 teaspoon saffron**
**1 3/4 cups chicken broth**
**1 cup long-grain white rice**

Over medium-low heat, sauté the garlic, onion, green bell pepper, and pimento in the olive oil until the vegetables caramelize. You may substitute pimento juice or chicken broth for the olive oil and simmer until the onions are transparent and the green bell peppers are soft. In a two-quart saucepan bring broth to a boil and add the rice and remaining ingredients. Add additional salt and pepper to taste. Cover the saucepan and cook over low heat for about 20 minutes.

*Makes 4 servings.*

# Jamaican Curried Goat

Delicious when served over a big mound of rice or rice and peas.

**2 pounds goat meat**
**2 teaspoons salt or to taste**
**3 tablespoons curry powder**
**1/2 teaspoon cumin**
**1/2 teaspoon black pepper**
**4 green onions, chopped**
**1 or 2 Scotch bonnet peppers, chopped, with or without seeds**
**2 cloves garlic, crushed**
**2 tablespoons butter**
**1/4 cup vegetable oil**
**3 cups beef broth**
**2 tomatoes, chopped**
**2 onions, sliced**
**4 to 5 potatoes, peeled and cut into bite-size pieces**
**Lemon juice**

Cut the goat meat into small pieces; place them in a bowl. Combine the salt, curry powder, cumin, and black pepper; mix well and use to season the goat meat. Stir in the green onions, Scotch bonnet peppers, and garlic, and set aside to marinate for at least 1 hour but preferably overnight. Brush onions, peppers, and garlic from the meat and fry it in the butter and oil over medium to medium-high heat until it is lightly browned.

Add enough broth to cover the meat and bring to a boil. Reduce the heat, cover the pan, and simmer until the meat is tender, adding more broth as necessary to permit the meat to boil freely without sticking. Add the sliced onions, potatoes, and stir in the seasonings in which the meat was marinated. Taste, adjust seasonings, cover the pot again, and allow goat to simmer another 15 to 20 minutes or until the broth approaches a stew-like consistency. However, it should not be too thick. Traditionally, the gravy is fairly thin so that you have lots to pour over the rice. Once the potatoes are cooked through, add a tablespoon or two of lemon juice.

Excellent when served with white rice, mango chutney, or fried plantains.

*Makes 4 to 6 servings.*

# Conch Stew

This tasty island stew is even better the second day. If you have difficulty finding conch meat, chicken, lobster, or shrimp may be substituted.

**2 1/2 pounds of conch meat**
**1/2 cup white wine vinegar**
**1 large onion, finely chopped**
**1 medium-size green pepper, finely chopped**
**2 cloves garlic, minced**
**2 tablespoons butter**
**2 tablespoons olive oil**
**2 tomatoes, peeled, seeded, and chopped**
**1/2 cup chicken broth**
**Dash of Tabasco sauce**
**1 tablespoon Maggi seasoning**

Clean, peel, and pound the conch well to tenderize. Next, wash it with the vinegar, cut it into bite-size pieces, and set aside.

Sauté the onions, green peppers, and garlic in butter and olive oil. Add the tomatoes, chicken broth, Tabasco, and Maggi seasoning. Simmer for approximately 20 minutes before adding the conch; cover and continue to cook until meat is tender, about 10 to 15 additional minutes.

*Makes 4 to 6 servings.*

# Excellent Pork Stew

**3 tablespoons vegetable oil**
**2 pounds pork tenderloin, cut into 1 1/2-inch pieces**
**1 large onion, chopped**
**2 tablespoons all purpose-flour**
**2 14 1/2-ounce cans beef broth**
**2 cups dry white wine**
**4 large potatoes cut lengthwise into quarters**
**1 large green bell pepper, chopped**
**3 large garlic cloves, chopped**
**1 tablespoon chopped fresh parsley**
**1 teaspoon thyme**
**1 teaspoon cumin**
**1/4 teaspoon chili powder**
**4 bay leaves**
**3 large carrots cut into 3/4-inch pieces**
**1/2 pound green beans, trimmed, halved**
**Salt and pepper to taste**
**Chopped fresh parsley**

Heat the oil in heavy large pot or Dutch oven over high heat. Add pork and onion and cook while stirring until the pork is brown on all sides and the onions begin to caramelize. Add flour and stir. Add beef broth and wine. Bring to a quick boil, reduce heat to a simmer and cook down until stock is reduced by half. Add remaining ingredients and continue to cook until meat is tender and the vegetables soft. Serve with a hearty homemade bread and salad.

*Makes 4 to 6 servings.*

# Clark Atlanta University

*If you're not living on the edge, you're taking up too much room.*

—African proverb

ON JULY 11, 1988, academic powerhouses Atlanta University and Clark College merged to form Clark Atlanta University (CAU). With this union CAU became the largest university in the Atlanta University System and the only one to grant graduate degrees. In addition, it became one of only two private, historically black universities in the United States to award doctorate degrees in more than five disciplines. Although traditionally identified as a historically black institution, today CAU is widely recognized as a national university as indicated by its classification as a Doctoral/Research–Intensive University by the Carnegie Foundation for the Advancement of Teaching in 2000 and its ranking as a national university by *U.S. News and World Report* in 2003. The only private historically black university in the nation to receive such a classification, Clark Atlanta University was also ranked as a "Top College for African Americans," in the January 2001 issue of *Black Enterprise*.

**Langston Hughes reception at Atlanta University, 1946.**
*(Archives and Special Collections: Robert Woodruff Library at the Atlanta University Center)*

**70th birthday celebration for Dr. W.E.B. Du Bois at Atlanta University, February 23, 1938.**
*(Archives and Special Collections: Robert Woodruff Library at the Atlanta University Center)*

These honors, especially its recognition as a national university, come as no surprise given its rich legacy of academic excellence from its parent institutions. Accepting as its mandate the motto of Atlanta University—"I'll Find a Way or Make One"—and that of Clark College—"Culture for Service"—Clark Atlanta stands alone as the nation's oldest historically black graduate institution.

Clark and Atlanta University have been strengthened both by the challenges they confronted individually and the partnership, which they formed in 1988. This dynamic union set Clark Atlanta University apart as one of the premiere universities of the twenty-first century. Justifiably proud of its past accomplishments, it continues to write new history and set even higher standards while charting a "Bold New Future."

**South Hall, Stone Hall, and North Hall.**
*(Archives and Special Collections: Robert Woodruff Library at the Atlanta University Center)*

# Breads, Biscuits, and Rolls

## Cornmeal Yeast Bread

Cornmeal isn't just for muffins and pan breads anymore.

**2 packages dry yeast**
**1/2 cup warm water (105–115°F)**
**3/4 cup warm evaporated milk (105–115°F)**
**1/3 cup butter, softened**
**1/3 cup sugar**
**1 teaspoon salt**
**1 egg, lightly beaten**
**1 cup all-purpose flour**
**3/4 cup yellow cornmeal**
**3 to 3 1/2 cups all-purpose flour**

Lightly oil two 8½ × 4½ × 3-inch loaf pans and set aside. Place yeast in a bowl with warm water and dissolve. Allow the yeast to proof for five minutes. Add the next four ingredients and stir until the butter melts. Next, add the egg, cornmeal, and flour. Use an electric mixer to beat at medium speed until the mixture is well blended. Gradually stir in sufficient flour to form a stiff dough.

Turn the dough out on a lightly floured surface and knead until the dough is smooth and elastic, approximately 10 minutes. Place in a lightly oiled mixing bowl, turning to grease the top. Cover the bowl with a clean tea-towel and allow the dough to rise in a warm (85°F) draft-free place for one hour or until doubled in bulk. Punch dough down and divide in half. Shape dough into two loaves and place into bread pans, cover with a clean tea-towel, and allow to rise until double in bulk, approximately 45 minutes. While bread is rising, preheat oven to 350°F. Bake bread at 350°F for 30 to 35 minutes or until the loaves sound hollow when lightly tapped with knuckles. Remove bread from the pans and cool on wire racks.

*Makes 2 loaves.*

# Yam Yeast Bread

**2 packages dry yeast**
**1½ cups very warm (110–115°F) water**
**¾ teaspoon sugar**
**5 to 6 cups unbleached white flour**
**3 teaspoons salt**
**½ teaspoon white pepper**
**⅛ teaspoon nutmeg**
**⅛ teaspoon mace**
**2 tablespoons butter, softened**
**1 cup cooked yam purée (from 1 to 2 yams)**
**1 egg, well beaten**

Grease and flour two 9 × 5-inch loaf pans and set aside. Place the yeast, warm water, and sugar in bowl and allow the yeast to dissolve. Combine 5 cups of the flour with the spices and gradually stir the flour mixture into the yeast mixture. Add the butter, yam purée, and additional flour, as necessary, to form a moist dough. Knead the dough for 10 to 15 minutes before placing it in a buttered bowl to rise. Cover the bowl with plastic and allow it to rise in a warm (75 to 80°F) draft-free place until doubled.

Punch dough down and let rise again about 45 minutes. Punch down, divide between the two prepared loaf pans, and allow dough to rise for another 45 minutes. Prepare the glaze by combining the egg with a teaspoon of water and mixing well. Brush the top of the bread with the glaze mixture before baking it in a preheated 425°F oven for 30 to 40 minutes or until the bottom of the loaf sounds hollow when rapped with knuckles. Cool on a rack at least an hour before slicing.

*Note:* If your room is drafty and your bread is having difficulty rising, place it on a heating pad set on low.

*Makes 2 loaves.*

# Cornmeal Rolls

With their unique Southern flair, the heady aroma of these fresh baked dinner rolls will beckon your family to the dinner table faster than you can say, "Dinner time."

**1¼ cups flour**
**¾ cup cornmeal**
**1 tablespoon sugar**
**½ teaspoon salt**
**1 tablespoon baking powder**
**2 tablespoons shortening**
**1 egg**
**½ cup milk**
**Melted butter**
**1 egg + 1 tablespoon water**

Preheat oven to 450°F. Sift together the flour, cornmeal, sugar, salt, and baking powder. Rub in the shortening with your fingertips. Add egg and milk, mix well, and roll out to a 1/4-inch thickness. Cut into rounds with a large cutter and brush with melted butter. Fold in half like a parker house roll, brush tops with egg white mixture, and dust with cornmeal. Press the fold gently and bake in preheated oven for 12 to 15 minutes.

*Makes 16 rolls.*

# Sour Cream Rolls

So deliciously light, they practically melt in your mouth. Almost impossible to resist, set them out and watch as they disappear.

**2 1/4 cups all-purpose flour, divided**
**2 tablespoons sugar**
**1 envelope yeast**
**3/4 teaspoon salt**
**3/4 cup sour cream**
**1/4 cup water**
**2 tablespoons butter**
**1 large egg**
**Melted butter**

In a large bowl, combine 1 cup of the flour, sugar, undissolved yeast, and salt. Heat the sour cream, water, and butter to 120 to 130°F. Gradually add the sour cream mixture to the flour mixture and beat with an electric mixer set at medium speed for two minutes. Add egg and remaining flour to form a soft batter. Spoon evenly into greased 2 1/2-inch muffin pans. Brush with melted butter, cover, and allow dough to rise until double in bulk, approximately 1 hour.

Bake in a preheated 400°F oven for 25 to 30 minutes.

*Makes 12 rolls.*

# Sour Cream Fan Rolls

**1 cup warm water (110–115°F)**
**2 tablespoons sugar**
**2 tablespoons active dry yeast**
**1/2 cup sugar, divided**
**2 cups warm sour cream (110–115°F)**
**2 eggs, lightly beaten**
**1/4 cup + 2 tablespoons melted butter**
**1 1/2 teaspoons salt**
**1/4 teaspoon baking powder**
**7 to 8 cups all-purpose flour**

Grease 18 muffin pan cups and set aside. Combine warm water with 2 tablespoons of sugar in a large mixing bowl and dissolve yeast in the sugar water. Allow yeast mixture to stand for 5 minutes. In a separate large bowl, combine the sour cream, eggs, butter, salt, and remaining sugar. Stir in the baking powder, yeast mixture, and four cups of flour until smooth. Mix in enough of the remaining flour to form a soft dough. Turn dough out onto a floured surface and knead the dough until it is smooth and elastic, approximately 7 to 8 minutes. Place the dough in a greased bowl, turning once to grease the top. Cover the bowl with a clean tea towel and allow to rise in a warm place until double in bulk, approximately 1 hour.

Punch dough down, turn out onto a lightly floured surface, and divide in half. Roll each half of dough into a 23-inch × 9-inch rectangle. Cut into 1 1/2-inch strips. Stack 5 strips together and cut the stacked strips into 1 1/2-inch pieces. Place each piece cut side up in a greased muffin cup. Cover with a clean tea towel and allow to rise until doubled in bulk, approximately 20 minutes. Preheat oven to 350°F. Bake in preheated oven for 20 to 25 minutes or until golden brown. Cool on wire racks.

*Makes 2 1/2 dozen rolls.*

# Potato Rosemary Rolls

Fragrant rosemary is the secret to these delicious dinner rolls that will have your friends and family asking for more.

**2 to 2 1/2 cups all-purpose flour, divided**
**1 1/2 tablespoons sugar**
**1 envelope quick rise yeast**
**1 1/4 teaspoons salt**
**1 teaspoon dried rosemary, crushed**
**1 cup milk**
**1/4 cup water**
**1/2 cup instant potatoes**
**2 tablespoons vegetable oil**
**1 egg, lightly beaten**
**Rosemary for topping**

In a large bowl combine 2/3 cup of flour, sugar, undissolved yeast, salt, and rosemary. Heat the milk, water, potato flakes, and oil to between 120 and 130°F. Gradually add the flour mixture to the milk mixture. Use an electric mixer to beat at medium speed for approximately 2 minutes. Stir in enough of the remaining flour to make a soft dough. Turn dough out onto a lightly floured surface and knead lightly until smooth and elastic, approximately 8 to 10 minutes. Cover and allow the dough to rest 10 minutes before dividing the dough into 12 equal pieces. Roll each piece into a 10 inch rope. Coil each rope, tucking the end under the roll. Place rolls two inches apart on a greased baking sheet. Cover and permit the rolls to rise in a warm (85°F) draft-free place for 1 hour or until doubled in bulk. Brush tops with egg mixture and sprinkle with additional rosemary. Bake at 375°F for 15 to 20 minutes or until done.

*Makes 12 rolls.*

# Whole Wheat Rolls

**3/4 cup milk**
**1/4 cup table cream**
**1/4 cup + 1 tablespoon sugar**
**1 teaspoon salt**
**1/4 cup shortening**
**1/4 cup warm water (105–110°F)**
**1 package dry yeast**
**1 egg, well beaten**
**2 cups whole wheat flour**
**1 1/2 cups all-purpose flour**
**Melted butter**

Preheat oven to 400°F. Grease a baking sheet and set aside. Scald milk and table cream; stir in sugar, salt, and shortening. Set aside and allow the milk mixture to cool to a lukewarm temperature. In a small bowl, combine warm water, yeast, and sugar; stir until the yeast and sugar are dissolved and set the yeast mixture aside to proof. Allow mixture to cool to lukewarm. Add the egg to the milk mixture and mix well. Add the proofed yeast and whole wheat flour; beat until the mixture is smooth. Next, add the all-purpose flour and mix until smooth. Place dough into a large greased bowl. Grease the top of the dough, cover with a clean tea towel, and allow it to rise in a warm (75 to 80°F) draft-free place until doubled. Punch dough down. Divide dough into two equal parts. Turn 1/2 of the dough onto a lightly floured board and roll into a circle approximately 10 inches in diameter. Cut the circle into 12 equal pie-shaped wedges. Roll each wedge tightly. Beginning at the widest end, roll the wedge toward the point and seal the points by wetting your finger tip and dampening the underside of the point. Gently press the point in place, rewet your finger, and rub it over the point until it seals. Place each crescent on the prepared baking sheet with the point beneath the roll. Curve each roll into the shape of a crescent and allow the rolls to rise 1 hour or until they double in bulk. Place rolls in preheated oven and bake for approximately 10 minutes or until the rolls are lightly browned. Serve with honey butter (see recipe below).

*Makes 2 dozen rolls.*

### HONEY BUTTER

**1/2 cup butter, softened**
**1/3 cup honey**

Combine butter and honey and beat until creamy. Serve at room temperature.

*Makes 6 to 10 servings.*

## Tea Biscuits

**2 cups all-purpose flour, sifted**
**3 teaspoons baking powder**
**1 teaspoon salt**
**1/2 cup shortening**
**1 egg, beaten**
**3/4 cup milk**

Preheat oven to 450°F. Sift together the flour, baking powder, and salt; cut in the shortening until the mixture resembles coarse cornmeal. Combine the egg and milk, mix well. Add to the flour mixture and mix until a smooth dough is formed. Turn the dough out onto a lightly floured surface and knead lightly. Roll out to a thickness of 1/2 inch and cut with a biscuit cutter. Place biscuits on an ungreased cookie sheet and bake in a 450°F oven for 12 to 15 minutes.

*Makes 12 biscuits.*

## Sweet Potato Pecan Biscuits

Serve these delicious biscuits piping hot, slathered with butter and sorghum syrup.

**3/4 cup cold mashed sweet potatoes**
**1/2 cup butter, melted and cooled**
**1/3 cup light brown sugar**

**Atlanta University faculty, 1890.**
*(Archives and Special Collections: Robert Woodruff Library at the Atlanta University Center)*

**½ cup buttermilk**
**2 cups self-rising flour**
**½ cup chopped pecans**

Preheat oven to 400°F. Combine sweet potatoes, butter, and brown sugar until well blended, and then stir in buttermilk. Stir the mixture until it is smooth. Add flour and stir until just moistened. Add the pecans to dough and turn it out on lightly floured surface. Knead the dough a few times until it holds together. Roll dough to ½-inch thickness and cut with floured 2-inch biscuit cutter. Bake on lightly greased baking sheet for 15 to 18 minutes.

*Makes about 18 biscuits.*

## James Weldon Johnson, Atlanta University '94

**Poet, composer, novelist, historian, lawyer, diplomat, and civil rights activist James Weldon Johnson is best remembered for penning the words to "Lift Every Voice and Sing," adopted by the NAACP as the Negro National Anthem. His equally talented brother Rosamond wrote the music for the now famous song.**

# Sweet Cornbread

**1 cup all-purpose flour**
**1 cup yellow cornmeal**
**1/3 cup granulated sugar**
**2 1/2 teaspoons baking powder**
**1/2 teaspoon salt**
**1/8 teaspoon nutmeg**
**2 large eggs**
**1 cup buttermilk**
**1/4 cup cooled, melted butter, divided**

Preheat oven to 400°F; butter an 8-inch square baking pan and set aside. Combine flour, cornmeal, sugar, baking powder, salt, and nutmeg in a bowl and mix well. In separate bowl, lightly beat eggs. Add buttermilk and 1/4 cup butter to the eggs and beat to blend. Combine the buttermilk mixture with the flour and mix until just moistened. Spoon the batter into a buttered baking pan and spread smooth.

Bake in the preheated oven for approximately 20 to 25 minutes or until the golden brown bread springs back when lightly pressed in the center and begins to pull from the sides of the pan. Cut bread into nine squares.

*Makes 9 servings.*

# Red Cornbread

**1 cup all-purpose flour**
**1 cup yellow cornmeal**
**1/3 cup granulated sugar**
**2 1/2 teaspoons baking powder**
**1/2 teaspoon salt**
**1 tablespoon paprika**
**2 large eggs**
**1 cup buttermilk**

**1/4 cup cooled, melted butter**
**1/2 cup canned roasted peppers**

Preheat oven to 400°F; butter an 8-inch square baking pan and set aside. In a bowl, mix flour, cornmeal, sugar, baking powder, salt, and paprika. In separate bowl, lightly beat eggs. Add buttermilk, butter, and roasted peppers to the eggs and beat to blend. Combine the buttermilk mixture with the flour and mix until just moistened. Spoon the batter into a buttered baking pan and spread smooth.

Bake in the preheated oven for approximately 20 to 25 minutes or until the golden brown bread springs back when lightly pressed in the center and begins to pull from the sides of the pan. Cut bread into nine squares.

*Makes 9 servings.*

# Basil Cornbread

**1 cup all-purpose flour**
**1 cup yellow cornmeal**
**1/3 cup granulated sugar**
**2 1/2 teaspoons baking powder**
**1/2 teaspoon salt**
**2 large eggs**
**1 cup buttermilk**
**1/4 cup cooled, melted butter**
**1 8 1/2-ounce can creamed corn**
**1/3 cup chopped fresh basil**

Preheat oven to 400°F; butter an 8-inch square baking pan and set aside. In a bowl, mix flour, cornmeal, sugar, baking powder, salt, and paprika. In a separate bowl, lightly beat eggs. Add buttermilk, melted butter, corn, and chopped basil to the eggs and beat to blend. Combine the buttermilk mixture with the flour and mix until just moistened. Spoon the batter into a buttered baking pan and spread smooth.

Bake in the preheated oven for approximately 20 to 25 minutes or until the golden brown bread springs back when lightly pressed in the center and begins to pull from the sides of the pan. Cut bread into squares.

*Makes 9 servings.*

# Curry Cornbread

**1 cup all-purpose flour**
**1 cup yellow cornmeal**
**1/3 cup granulated sugar**
**2 1/2 teaspoons baking powder**
**1/2 teaspoon salt**
**1 tablespoon curry powder**
**2 large eggs**
**1 cup buttermilk**
**1/4 cup cooled, melted butter**

Preheat oven to 400°F; butter an 8-inch square baking pan and set aside. In a bowl, mix flour, cornmeal, sugar, baking powder, salt, and curry powder. In separate bowl, lightly beat eggs. Add buttermilk, melted butter, and roasted peppers to the eggs and beat to blend. Combine the buttermilk mixture with the flour and mix until just moistened. Spoon the batter into a buttered baking pan and spread smooth.

Bake in the preheated oven for approximately 20 to 25 minutes or until the golden brown bread springs back when lightly pressed in the center and begins to pull from the sides of the pan. Cut bread into nine squares.

*Makes 9 servings.*

## Dr. Ralph David Abernathy

The son of a farmer, Ralph Abernathy was born in 1926 in Lindon, Alabama. He became an ordained Baptist minister in 1948 and two years later graduated with a B.S. in mathematics from Alabama State University. In 1951, he earned his M.A. in sociology from Atlanta University. He accepted a pastorate at First Baptist Church in Montgomery, where he met Dr. Martin Luther King, Jr. Their relationship would be solidified by unfolding civil rights events in a deeply segregated city.

On December 1, 1955, Rosa Parks, a tired tailor's assistant, refused to give up her seat to a white man and move to the back of the bus. Following her arrest, Abernathy and King organized the year-long Montgomery bus boycott. For more than a year 17,000 black citizens of Montgomery either walked to work or received rides from the few members of the black community who owned cars. Loss of revenue and a decision by the Supreme Court affirming the U.S. District Court's ruling that segregation on buses was

Atlanta University System baccalaureate, 1950.

*(Archives and Special Collections: Robert Woodruff Library at the Atlanta University Center)*

**unconstitutional brought the boycott to an end on December 20, 1956.**

**Following the boycott's successful conclusion, Abernathy and King continued working together and in 1957, together with Fred Shuttlesworth and Bayard Rustin, they created the Southern Christian Leadership Conference (SCLC) to organize nonviolent protest. King served as president and Abernathy as secretary-treasurer. In 1961, Abernathy moved to Atlanta and was also appointed vice-president of the SCLC. In May 1968, he directed the Poor People's March in Washington and that same year helped organize the Atlanta sanitation workers' strike. Over the next few years Abernathy was arrested 19 times. He continued working closely with King until the latter's assassination in 1968.**

**In 1977 Abernathy resigned from the Southern Christian Leadership Conference and served as a pastor of a Baptist church in Atlanta. He later made an unsuccessful run for a Georgia congressional seat. His autobiography, *And the Walls Came Tumbling Down,* was published in 1989, the year before he died.**

## Sour Cream Cornbread

Cornbread, any way you make it, is a tasty companion to any meal, but it is especially tasty with soups and stews.

**1 cup all-purpose flour**
**3/4 cup yellow cornmeal**
**1/4 cup + 1 teaspoon sugar**
**1/2 teaspoon salt**
**1/2 teaspoon baking soda**
**1 cup sour cream**
**1/4 cup table cream**
**1 egg, slightly beaten**
**2 tablespoons melted butter**

Preheat oven to 425°F; lightly grease an 8-inch square pan and set aside. In a large mixing bowl combine the dry ingredients and mix well to blend. In a separate bowl combine the remaining ingredients and mix well. Fold into the dry ingredients and mix well to blend. Pour into the pan and bake in preheated oven for 20 minutes or until golden brown and a toothpick inserted in the center comes out clean. Remove from oven, cut into 9 squares, and serve warm.

*Makes 9 squares.*

# Cake Cornbread

**1 1/4 cups sugar**
**1/4 cup honey**
**2 eggs**
**1/2 cup butter, softened**
**1 1/4 cups half and half**
**3/4 cup water**
**2 cups white cornmeal**
**2 cups flour**
**1 tablespoon baking powder**
**3/4 teaspoon salt**
**Pinch of nutmeg**

Preheat oven to 375°F; butter a 9 × 13-inch baking pan and set aside. Combine sugar, honey, butter, eggs, half and half, and water in a large bowl and mix to blend. In a separate bowl mix together the cornmeal, flour, baking powder, salt and nutmeg. Add the milk mixture and stir thoroughly. The mixture should be slightly lumpy. Pour into the buttered baking pan. Bake for 25 to 30 minutes or until golden brown on top. Serve piping hot, with butter.

*Makes 12 servings.*

**Atlanta University commencement, 1961.**
*(Archives and Special Collections: Robert Woodruff Library at the Atlanta University Center)*

## Whitney Young

Educator, social engineer, and civil rights leader Whitney Moore Young, Jr., was born in Lincoln Ridge, Kentucky, in 1921 to a family considered part of the black educated elite. His father presided over Lincoln Institute, the black boarding school where his mother taught and that his son attended. The family lived in a simple two-story wooden house on the campus until Young was 15 years old.

In 1944, after studying engineering for two years at MIT, he enlisted in the army and was sent to Europe, where he joined an all-black regiment led by a white captain. Often called upon to diffuse racial tension between the captain and his troops, Young honed his legendary skills as a mediator between the races. He later said, "It was my Army experience that decided me on getting into the race relations field after the war. Not just because I saw the problems, but because I saw the potentials, too. I grew up with a basic belief in the inherent decency of human beings."

After the war Young entered the University of Minnesota where he earned an MSW and became a university lecturer. In 1954 he was named dean of the School of Social Work at Atlanta University, in which position he supported an alumni-led boycott of the Georgia Conference of Social Welfare, which had a poor record of placing African Americans in good jobs. At the same time, he joined the NAACP and rose to become state president.

In 1960, Young received a Rockefeller grant to study for a year at Harvard University. Subsequently, he was appointed to succeed Lester B. Ganger as president of the National Urban League. He immediately began revitalizing the Urban League, turning it from a relatively passive civil rights organization into one that aggressively fought for justice. He infused the organization with money, through his connections with funding sources like the Rockefeller family. Its annual budget increased from $325,000.00 to $6,100,000; the number of employees increased from 38 to 1600. He also initiated alternative education programs such as Street Academy, to prepare dropouts for college, and New Thrust, directed at empowering local black leaders to identify and solve community problems. In addition to pushing for federal aid to cities, Young also participated in all major civil rights demonstrations, including the March on Washington on August 28, 1963, which he was instrumental in bringing to fruition. A close adviser to Presidents Kennedy and Johnson, in 1968, he was honored by President Johnson with the nation's highest award, the Presidential Medal of Freedom.

# Jalapeño Corn Muffins

1 cup all-purpose flour
1 cup yellow cornmeal
1/3 cup granulated sugar
2 1/2 teaspoons baking powder
1/2 teaspoon salt
1/4 teaspoon paprika

**2 large eggs**
**1 cup buttermilk**
**1/4 cup cooled, melted butter**
**1/2 cup jalapeño jelly**

Preheat oven to 400°F; butter 12 2 1/2 inch muffin cups. In a bowl, mix flour, cornmeal, sugar, baking powder, salt, and paprika. In separate bowl, lightly beat eggs. Add buttermilk and melted butter to eggs; beat to blend. Combine the buttermilk mixture with the flour and mix until just moistened.

Evenly divide half of the batter into the buttered muffin cups. Top the batter with 2 teaspoons of jalapeño jelly. Evenly divide the remaining batter amongst the cups and place in the preheated oven. Bake for approximately 20 to 25 minutes or until a golden brown muffin springs back when lightly pressed in the center and begins to pull from the sides of the muffin pan.

*Makes 12 muffins.*

# Peach and Poppy Seed Muffins

**2/3 cup puréed peaches**
**1 teaspoon baking soda**
**10 tablespoons butter, softened**
**1 cup sugar**
**2 eggs**
**1 1/4 cups flour**
**1/4 teaspoon salt**
**1/2 teaspoon vanilla extract**
**3 tablespoons poppy seeds**

Preheat oven to 350°F. Grease muffin tins for a dozen muffins. Stir baking soda into puréed peaches. They will foam up. In a separate bowl, cream butter with sugar. When mixture is smooth, add eggs, one at a time. Alternately add flour and peach purée to the butter mixture, then add salt, vanilla extract, and poppy seeds.

Fill each muffin cup nearly to the top. Bake 20 to 25 minutes or until a toothpick or cake tester inserted in one of the muffins comes out clean.

*Makes 12 large muffins.*

## Blueberry Muffins

Blueberries are a great source of vitamin C, iron, and fiber, and they contain only 80 calories per cup. The harvest season in Georgia is late May through mid-July. When shopping for blueberries look for plump, firm blueberries that are a light powdery blue-gray color.

**2 cups all-purpose flour**
**2 cups quick oats**
**1 cup dark brown sugar**
**1 teaspoon salt**
**2¼ teaspoons cinnamon**
**2 cups milk**
**2 eggs, lightly beaten**
**3 tablespoons vegetable oil**
**4 cups blueberries**

Preheat oven to 425°F and line large muffin tins with paper muffin cups. In a large measuring bowl, combine the dry ingredients. Combine the liquid ingredients in a separate bowl and mix to blend. Add to the dry ingredients, and stir just until dry ingredients are moistened. Fold in blueberries. Fill muffin cups ¾ full. Bake 25 minutes. These muffins may be frozen after they have cooled.

*Makes 16 large muffins.*

# Fruit Breads

## Banana Bread

**5 tablespoons butter (no substitutes)**
**1/2 cup sugar**
**1/2 cup firmly packed dark brown sugar**
**1 large egg**
**2 egg whites**
**1 1/2 teaspoons vanilla extract**
**1 1/2 cups mashed very ripe bananas**
**1 3/4 cups all-purpose flour**
**1 teaspoon baking soda**
**1/2 teaspoon salt**
**3/4 teaspoon ground cinnamon**
**1/8 teaspoon allspice**
**1/4 teaspoon baking powder**
**1/2 cup heavy cream**
**1/3 cup chopped walnuts**

Preheat oven to 350°F; grease and flour a 9 × 5-inch loaf pan and set aside. Place the butter in a large bowl and beat it with an electric mixer set at medium speed until light and fluffy. Gradually add the sugars, beating well after each addition. Next, add the egg, egg whites, and vanilla extract; beat until well blended. Add the mashed bananas and beat on high speed for 30 seconds. In a separate bowl, combine the flour, baking soda, salt, spices, and baking powder, mix to combine before adding the flour mixture to the banana mixture alternately with cream, ending with flour. Add the walnuts and mix well. Spoon mixture into the prepared loaf pan and bake in the preheated oven for 1 hour and 15 minutes or until a tester inserted into the center comes out clean. Allow bread to sit for 10 minutes before turning it out on a wire rack to cool.

*Makes 1 loaf.*

## Peach Loaf

**1½ cups all-purpose flour**
**½ teaspoon salt**
**½ teaspoon baking soda**
**¼ teaspoon cinnamon**
**1 cup sugar**
**2 eggs, well beaten**
**½ cup vegetable oil**
**1½ cups peeled and pitted peaches, coarsely chopped**
**1 teaspoon vanilla extract**
**½ cup chopped pecans**

Preheat oven to 350°F; grease and flour a 9 × 5-inch loaf pan and set aside. Combine the flour, salt, baking soda, cinnamon, and sugar and mix well. Form a well in the middle of the flour mixture and add the eggs and oil to it. Mix just until the dry ingredients are moistened. Add the peaches, vanilla extract, and nuts. Mix to combine and pour into prepared baking pan. Place in the preheated oven and bake for 1 hour and 30 minutes or until a tester inserted in the center comes out clean. Allow the loaf to rest for 10 minutes before turning it out on a wire rack to cool.

*Makes 1 loaf.*

# Pumpkin Bread

3 cups sugar
1 cup vegetable oil
4 eggs, beaten
1 teaspoon vanilla extract
1 16-ounce can pumpkin purée or pie filling
3 1/2 cups flour
2 teaspoons baking soda
1 teaspoon salt
1 teaspoon baking powder
1 1/4 teaspoons nutmeg
1 teaspoon allspice
1/4 teaspoon cloves
1 1/4 teaspoons cinnamon
2/3 cup water

Preheat oven to 350°F; grease and flour two 9 × 5 loaf pans and set aside. Cream the sugar and oil together. Add the eggs, vanilla extract, and pumpkin purée and mix well. Sift together the remaining dry ingredients and add them to the pumpkin mixture alternately with the water. Spoon mixture into the prepared pans and bake in preheated oven for 1 1/2 hours or until a tester inserted in the center comes out clean. Allow the bread to rest for 10 minutes before removing it from the pan to cool.

*Makes 2 loaves.*

# Pumpkin Raisin Pecan Bread

2 cups all-purpose flour, sifted
2 teaspoons baking powder
1/2 teaspoon baking soda
3/4 teaspoon salt
1 teaspoon ground cinnamon

1/2 teaspoon ground nutmeg
1/8 teaspoon allspice
1 cup canned pumpkin
1 cup sugar
1/2 cup evaporated milk
1 teaspoon vanilla extract
1/8 teaspoon almond extract
2 eggs, beaten
1/4 cup butter, softened
1/2 cup chopped pecans
1/2 cup raisins

Preheat oven to 350°F; grease and flour a 9 × 5-inch loaf pan and set aside. Combine flour, baking powder, baking soda, salt, and spices in a large bowl. In a separate bowl, combine the pumpkin, sugar, milk, extracts, and eggs and mix well. Add the pumpkin mixture and the butter to the dry ingredients and mix until well blended. Add pecans and raisins and mix to combine. Spoon the mixture into the prepared loaf pan and bake in the preheated oven from 45 to 55 minutes or until a tester inserted into the center comes out clean.

*Makes 8 servings.*

## Strawberry Nut Bread

3 eggs, well beaten
2 cups sugar
1 1/2 cups oil
1 1/4 teaspoons vanilla extract
3 cups flour
1 teaspoon baking soda
3/4 teaspoon salt
3/4 teaspoon cinnamon
Pinch of allspice

**Cheerleading.**
*(Archives and Special Collections: Robert Woodruff Library at the Atlanta University Center)*

**2 cups strawberries, and juice**
**1 cup chopped pecans**

Combine the eggs, sugar, oil, and vanilla extract; mix well. In a separate bowl, sift together the dry ingredients. Add the strawberries, strawberry juice and nuts, mixing well after each addition. Bake in 2 or 3 loaf pans at 350°F for 1 hour or until a tester inserted in the center comes out clean.

*Makes 2 to 3 loaves.*

## Professor William H. Crogman

William H. Crogman
*(Archives and Special Collections: Robert Woodruff Library at the Atlanta University Center)*

**Professor William H. Crogman, Litt.D., was born in the West Indies in 1841. Orphaned at age 12, he left the islands at 14 with B. L. Boomer, at that time first mate on a sailing vessel. Soon after arriving at Boomer's home in Massachusetts, young Crogman was**

enrolled in the district school, where he performed well. However, Crogman soon returned to the sea, following Boomer and his brother, who was the ship's captain, on their sea voyages around the world for the next ten years.

In 1866, Boomer, aware that Crogman possessed a strong intellect, suggested that he save his money to pursue an academic education. Following that advice, Crogman entered Pierce Academy, in Middleboro, Massachusetts, two years later.

After completing his studies at the academy, he went south and devoted the remainder of his life to the elevation of his people. He entered Atlanta University in the fall of 1873, where he met his future wife, and graduated with the university's first class in 1876. That September, 1876, he accepted a position on the faculty of Clark University, where he taught Latin and Greek, eventually chairing the department. He served as the only secretary of the Boards of

William H. Crogman Chapel

*(Archives and Special Collections: Robert Woodruff Library at the Atlanta University Center)*

William H. Crogman Cottage
*(Archives and Special Collections: Robert Woodruff Library at the Atlanta University Center)*

Trustees of Gammon Theological Seminary and of Clark University for many years. He served as president of Clark University for seven years, growing the school in numbers and strength. He was the superintendent of the Sunday school at Clark for 29 years, in which position he is reputed to have never been tardy. The author of several books, Crogman was also a much sought-after speaker. Dr. Crogman was the first individual to receive the degree of Doctor of Letters from Atlanta University.

At the 1921 commencement season, when Dr. Crogman retired from active teaching, the Carnegie Foundation awarded him a lifetime pension.

# *Hot from the Oven: Desserts*

## Peach Cake

**2 cups sugar**
**3 eggs, well beaten**
**1 1/2 cups vegetable oil**
**3 cups cake flour**
**1 teaspoon baking soda**
**3/4 teaspoon salt**
**2 teaspoons ground cinnamon**
**1/8 teaspoon nutmeg**
**Pinch of allspice**
**1 teaspoon vanilla extract**
**3 cups slightly firm ripe peaches, peeled and sliced thin**

Preheat oven to 350°F; grease and flour a 10-inch bundt pan and set aside. Combine sugar, eggs, and vegetable oil in a large mixing bowl and beat well. In a separate bowl sift together the flour, baking soda, salt, and remaining spices. Stir flour mixture 1 cup at a time into the sugar mixture. Beat well after each addition. Stir in the vanilla and peaches. Spoon the mixture into the bundt pan and bake for 1 hour or until a tester inserted into the center comes out clean. Allow cake to rest 10 minutes before turning out on a cake rack to cool. Drizzle glaze (recipe follows) over cooled cake.

*Makes 10 to 12 servings.*

### Glaze

**1/4 cup melted butter**
**2 cups powdered sugar, sifted**

**2 tablespoons heavy cream**
**1/4 teaspoon almond extract**

Combine the powdered sugar and melted butter; mix well. Add remaining ingredients and stir until the mixture is smooth and satiny.

*Makes about 2 cups.*

## Pecan Spice Cake

**1 cup shortening**
**2 cups sugar**
**4 eggs, beaten**
**3 cups sifted flour**
**1 teaspoon baking powder**
**3/4 teaspoon ground cinnamon**
**1/2 teaspoon ground cloves**
**Pinch of nutmeg**
**1 cup buttermilk**
**2 cups chopped pecans**
**Powdered sugar**

Preheat oven to 350°F; grease and flour a bundt or tube pan and set aside. Beat shortening with an electric mixer for 2 to 3 minutes before gradually adding the sugar and beating until the mixture is light and fluffy. Slowly add the eggs while continuing to beat the mixture until well blended. In a separate bowl sift together the dry ingredients 3 times before adding it to the shortening mixture. Alternate flour mixture with buttermilk and beat after each addition. Stir in the pecans and pour the batter into the prepared baking pan. Place pan into the oven and bake for 1 hour or until a tester inserted into the center comes out clean. When cake is sufficiently cool, lightly dust it with powdered sugar.

*Makes 12 servings.*

# Sweet Potato Cake with Pineapple Filling

**1 1/2 cups vegetable oil**
**2 cups sugar**
**4 eggs, separated (reserve whites)**
**4 tablespoons hot water**
**2 1/2 cups cake flour**
**3 teaspoons baking powder**
**1/4 teaspoon salt**
**1 1/4 teaspoons ground cinnamon**
**3/4 teaspoon ground nutmeg**
**Pinch ground allspice**
**1 1/2 cups peeled and grated raw sweet potato**
**1 1/2 teaspoons vanilla extract**
**1/8 teaspoon almond extract**
**1/2 cup coarsely chopped pecans**
**Cream cheese frosting**
**Grated coconut**

Preheat oven to 350°F; grease and flour three 8-inch cake pans and set aside. Combine the oil and sugar in a large mixing bowl and beat until well blended. Add egg yolks one at a time and beat well after each addition. Add hot water and mix well. In a separate bowl sift together the dry ingredients and gradually add to the egg mixture while continuing to beat. Stir in the potatoes, pecans, and extracts. Beat egg whites until stiff peaks form and gently fold into the batter. Place cake in the oven and bake for 25 to 30 minutes or until a tester inserted into the center comes out clean. Allow cakes to cool slightly before removing them from pans. While cakes are still slightly warm, spread the pineapple filling (recipe follows) between the layers. Allow the cake to cool completely and frost with cream cheese frosting (recipe follows). Garnish top of cake with coconut.

*Makes 8 to 10 servings.*

### PINEAPPLE FILLING

**3 tablespoons cake flour**
**1/2 cup sugar**
**1 20-ounce can crushed pineapple, undrained**
**1/8 teaspoon salt**
**2 tablespoons butter**

Combine flour and sugar in a small saucepan; mix until flour dissolves and no lumps are present; add pineapple, salt, and butter. Cook over medium heat, stirring constantly, until mixture is thickened. Cool. Cover to prevent skin from forming on top of filling and cool before using to fill the cake.

*Makes 2 2/3 cups.*

### CREAM CHEESE FROSTING

**3/4 cup unsalted butter, softened at room temperature**
**1 12-ounce package cream cheese, softened at room temperature**
**6 3/4 cups confectioner's sugar**
**2 teaspoons vanilla extract**
**16 ounces grated coconut**

Cream together the butter and cream cheese until the mixture is light and fluffy. Gradually add powdered sugar while continuing to beat. Stir in the vanilla extract and coconut, and mix well.

*Makes about 4 cups.*

## Peanut Butter Cake with Creamy Chocolate Amaretto Frosting

**3/4 cup butter, softened at room temperature**
**3/4 cup creamy peanut butter**
**2 cups firmly packed brown sugar**
**3 eggs, at room temperature**

**1½ teaspoons vanilla extract**
**2½ cups cake flour**
**1 tablespoon baking powder**
**1 teaspoon salt**
**1 cup evaporated milk**
**½ cup chopped peanuts without skins**
**½ cup miniature chocolate chips**

Preheat oven to 350°F. Grease a 13 × 9 × 2-inch baking pan and set aside. Remove butter and eggs from the refrigerator approximately three hours before use. Combine butter and peanut butter and beat until well blended. Add sugar and cream the ingredients together until light and fluffy. Next, add the eggs, beating well after each addition. Add extract. Sift together flour, baking powder, and salt; add to butter mixture by alternating with additions of milk. Beat well after each addition. Spoon the batter into the prepared baking pan and bake for 40 to 45 minutes or until a tester inserted into the center comes out clean. Cool cake at room temperature before frosting with Creamy Chocolate Amaretto Frosting (recipe follows) and sprinkling with chopped peanuts and chocolate chips.

*Makes 12 servings.*

## CREAMY CHOCOLATE AMARETTO FROSTING

**1 6-ounce package semisweet chocolate morsels**
**⅓ cup table cream**
**1¾ cups confectioner's sugar**
**3 tablespoons amaretto liqueur**

Combine chocolate morsels and table cream in a medium-size saucepan and heat on low, stirring constantly, until the morsels are melted. Allow to cool 5 minutes before stirring in the powdered sugar, and amaretto and beat until the mixture is smooth.

*Makes about 2 cups.*

# Buttermilk Pound Cake

**2 sticks butter, softened**
**3 cups sugar**
**5 large eggs**
**1 1/4 teaspoons vanilla extract**
**3 cups flour**
**1/2 teaspoon baking powder**
**3/4 cup buttermilk**

Preheat oven to 325°F; grease and flour a 12-cup Bundt or tube pan and set aside. In a large bowl cream the butter until light and fluffy. Gradually add the sugar and continue beating until light and fluffy. Add the eggs one at a time, and beat well after each addition. Add vanilla extract and mix to blend. In a separate bowl sift together the flour and the baking powder. Alternate between gradually adding the flour mixture and the buttermilk to the butter mixture, and beat after each addition. Pour into the prepared pan and bake for one hour.

*Makes 10 to 12 servings.*

# Coconut Cream Cake with Lemon Filling

**3 cups sugar**
**1/2 pound butter (2 sticks)**
**6 eggs**
**2 1/2 teaspoons vanilla extract**
**1 1/4 teaspoons vanilla extract**
**3 cups cake flour**
**2 teaspoons baking powder**
**1 cup whipping cream**

Cream the butter and sugar until light and fluffy. Add eggs one at a time, beating well after each addition. Add vanilla extract. In a separate bowl, sift together cake flour and baking powder. Add the flour mixture to the butter mixture alternately with the whipping cream, beating well after each addition. Divide batter among the three prepared 9-inch cake pans, place in a preheated oven and bake for 25 minutes or until a tester inserted into the center comes out clean. Spread lemon filling (recipe follows) between slightly warm layers; allow the cake to cool before frosting with cream cheese frosting (recipe follows).

## LEMON FILLING

**1 tablespoon grated lemon zest**
**1/2 cup fresh lemon juice**
**1 tablespoon cornstarch**
**6 tablespoons butter**
**3/4 cup white sugar**
**4 egg yolks, beaten**

Combine lemon zest, lemon juice, and cornstarch in a medium-sized saucepan and mix until smooth. Add the butter and sugar, and bring mixture to boil over medium heat. Boil for 1 minute, stirring constantly to prevent scorching. Remove from heat and set aside. In small bowl, beat egg yolks with a wire whisk until smooth. Whisk in a small amount of the hot lemon mixture. Pour the egg mixture into the saucepan and return to heat while beating the hot lemon mixture rapidly. Reduce heat to low; cook, stirring constantly, for 5 minutes, or until thick (but do not boil).

Pour mixture into medium size bowl and press plastic wrap onto the surface of the lemon filling mixture to keep skin from forming as it cools. Cool to room temperature. Refrigerate 3 hours.

*Makes about 1 1/2 cups.*

# Banana Nut Cake

**½ cup softened butter**
**1½ cups sugar**
**3 eggs (reserve the whites)**
**1 teaspoon vanilla extract**
**1 cup mashed bananas**
**¼ cup boiling water**
**½ cup chopped pecans**
**2 cups flour**
**1 teaspoon baking powder**
**¼ teaspoon salt**
**¼ teaspoon ground nutmeg**
**1 teaspoon baking soda**
**¼ cup buttermilk**

In a large bowl cream together the butter and sugar until light and fluffy. Add egg yolks one at a time, beating after each addition. Add vanilla extract and the mashed bananas; mix well. Pour boiling water over the pecans and set aside. In a separate bowl sift together the flour, baking powder, salt, and ground nutmeg and set aside. In a separate bowl, combine baking soda and buttermilk. Add the flour mixture to the banana mixture alternately with buttermilk mixture. Beat well after each addition. Add the pecans. Beat egg whites until stiff peaks form and fold into the batter. Bake for 30 to 35 minutes and allow it to cool completely before spreading it with banana filling and frosting (recipe follows).

*Makes 8 to 12 servings.*

### BANANA FILLING

**½ cup softened butter**
**1 pound powdered sugar**
**½ cup mashed bananas**
**½ cup chopped pecans**
**1 tablespoon pineapple juice**

Mix butter and powdered sugar until creamy. Add bananas, nuts, and juice. Mix well and spread between cooled cake layers.

*Makes about 3 1/2 cups.*

### Cream Cheese Frosting

**3/4 cup unsalted butter, softened at room temperature**
**1 12-ounce package cream cheese, softened at room temperature**
**6 3/4 cups confectioner's sugar**
**2 teaspoons vanilla extract**
**16 ounces grated coconut**

Cream together the butter and cream cheese until the mixture is light and fluffy. Gradually add confectioner's sugar while continuing to beat. Stir in the vanilla extract and mix well. Garnish the top and sides of the cake with grated coconut.

*Makes about 5 cups.*

## Georgia Peach and Praline Pie

**1 9-inch unbaked pie shell**
**1 teaspoon all-purpose flour**
**1/3 cup all-purpose flour, divided**
**1/4 cup sugar**
**1/4 teaspoon salt**
**1/3 teaspoon ground nutmeg**
**1/8 teaspoon cinnamon**
**1/8 teaspoon allspice**
**1/2 cup light corn syrup**
**3 eggs**
**3 cups fresh peach slices, chopped**
**1/4 cup butter, melted**
**1/4 cup firmly packed brown sugar**

**2 tablespoons butter, softened**
**1/2 cup coarsely chopped pecans**
**Whipped cream (optional)**

Sprinkle 1 teaspoon flour over pie crust; set aside. Combine 3 tablespoons flour, sugar, salt, spices, corn syrup and eggs in a mixing bowl; beat at medium speed with an electric mixer for 1 minute. Fold in peaches and the melted butter. Pour mixture into pie crust. Mix together the remaining flour and brown sugar in another bowl. Using a pastry blender, cut in 2 tablespoons of the softened butter until the mixture resembles coarse crumbs; add chopped pecans and stir. Sprinkle crumb mixture evenly over peach filling. Bake at 375°F for 45 to 50 minutes or until center of pie is set (cover crust edges with foil after 35 minutes to prevent overbrowning).

Eat it warmed, with a dollop of whipped cream, and it's a small slice of heaven!

*Makes 8 servings.*

# Peach Crumb Pie

One of the many pleasures of summer in the South is the abundance and variety of fresh fruit. Treat your family to this summer delight any time of year. Preserved peaches allow you to enjoy delicious peach pie year 'round, well after the season has passed.

**3/4 cup sugar**
**2 tablespoons butter**
**1/4 cup flour**
**1 teaspoon ground cinnamon**
**Unbaked pie shell**
**1 canned peach halves, reserve the syrup**
**1/4 cup peach syrup**
**2 tablespoons lemon juice**

Combine the sugar and butter and mix well. In a separate bowl combine the flour and cinnamon and mix well. Add the butter mixture to the bowl containing the flour, and cut it into the flour until a crumbly mixture resembling cornmeal is formed. Sprinkle half of this mixture on the bottom of the pie shell. Combine the peaches, syrup, and lemon juice, mix well, and pour over the crumb mixture in the pie pan. Cover with the remaining crumbs. Place in preheated 375°F oven and bake until the crust is well browned, approximately 1 hour.

# Georgia Pecan Pie

Georgia will be on your mind and on the mind of everyone who samples this delectable pie.

**3 eggs**
**2 tablespoons sugar**
**2 tablespoons flour**
**2 cups dark Karo syrup**
**1 teaspoon vanilla extract**
**1/4 teaspoon salt**
**1 1/4 cup pecan halves**
**1 unbaked pie shell**

Beat the eggs until light and set aside. In a separate bowl, combine the sugar and flour, mix well, add to the eggs, and beat to combine. Add the Karo, vanilla, salt, and pecans, mix well, and pour into the uncooked pie shell. Bake at 425°F for 10 minutes, reduce heat to 325°F, and continue baking for an additional 45 minutes.

*Makes 8 servings.*

# Georgia Pecan Pie II

**3 eggs, whole**
**1 cup dark Karo syrup**
**1 cup granulated sugar**
**1 to 2 cups chopped pecans**
**6 tablespoons butter, room temperature**
**1 teaspoon vanilla**
**1 pinch salt**
**1 unbaked pie shell**

Mix ingredients and pour into unbaked pie shell. Bake until filling is set, pecans look toasted, and pie crust is nicely browned. Serve pie either cold or slightly warm.

*Makes 8 servings.*

# Apple Crumb Pie

Nothing makes one's home feel quite as cozy as the fragrance of apples, cinnamon, and vanilla wafting through it on a crisp, autumn day.

**2 quarts apples, peeled, cored and thickly sliced**
**1 teaspoon salt**
**1 teaspoon cinnamon**
**1 teaspoon nutmeg**
**2 teaspoons vanilla extract**
**1/2 cup brown sugar**
**1/2 cup flour**
**1 teaspoon cinnamon**
**1/4 cup butter**
**unbaked pie shell**

Preheat oven to 425°F. Combine the apples and the next 4 ingredients and mix well and set aside. In a separate bowl, combine the remaining ingredients except the pie shell and mix to form crumbs. Spoon apples into the pie shell, mound slightly higher in the middle. Spread crumb mixture evenly over the top of the pie, and place in the preheated oven. Bake until apples are softened, approximately 1 hour.

*Makes 8 servings.*

## Coconut Cream Pie

**1 cup white sugar**
**1/2 cup all-purpose flour**
**1/4 teaspoon salt**
**3 cups milk**
**4 egg yolks, lightly beaten**
**3 tablespoons butter**
**2 teaspoons vanilla extract**
**1/8 teaspoon almond extract**
**1 cup flaked coconut**
**1 9-inch pie shell, baked**
**Whipped cream**

Combine sugar, flour, and salt in a medium-size saucepan. While constantly stirring over a medium heat, gradually add the milk. Continue cooking and stirring over medium heat until the mixture is thick and bubbly. Reduce heat to low and cook 2 minutes more. Remove the pan from heat.

Gradually stir 1 cup of the hot milk mixture into the beaten egg yolks, then return this mixture to the saucepan and recombine with the rest of the milk mixture. Bring to a gentle boil. Cook and stir 2 minutes before removing the pan from heat.

Add butter, vanilla extract, almond extract, and coconut into the hot mixture, and stir to combine. Pour the hot filling into the baked pie crust. Thoroughly chill and garnish with whipped cream prior to serving.

*Makes 8 servings.*

**Andrew Young at Clark College commencement, 1975.**
*(Archives and Special Collections: Robert Woodruff Library at the Atlanta University Center)*

# Fresh Strawberry Pie

As beautiful to look at as it is to eat. Serve up a delicious slice of summer with this rich, luscious strawberry filled pie. Strawberries do not ripen after they are picked, so be sure to select fully ripened, ruby red berries with fresh looking caps.

**1½ quarts fresh strawberries, washed and hulled**
**3 tablespoons cornstarch**
**1 cup sugar**
**2 tablespoons lemon juice**
**1 9-inch baked pie shell**
**Whipped cream**

Separate out approximately half of the best strawberries. In a large mixing bowl, mash the remaining strawberries, add the cornstarch and sugar to the mashed strawberries, place mixture in a saucepan, bring to a boil and cook until the liquid is thick and clear, approximately 3 minutes. Remove from the heat and stir in the lemon juice. Cool the strawberry mixture and add the reserved strawberries, cutting the larger ones in half if necessary (save a few to garnish your pie). Pour into pie shell, and chill thoroughly. Garnish with whipped cream immediately before serving.

*Makes 8 servings.*

## Jamaican Rum Cake

**1 pound butter or margarine, softened**
**1 pound dark brown sugar**
**1 dozen eggs**
**1 pound flour**
**2¼ teaspoons vanilla extract**
**2 teaspoons burnt sugar (found in Caribbean markets)**
**2 teaspoons baking powder**
**2 teaspoons baking soda**
**1¼ teaspoons ground cinnamon**
**¼ teaspoon ground nutmeg**
**⅛ teaspoon ground allspice**
**2 cups fruit mixture (recipe follows)**
**Rum**

Prepare the fruit mixture one month in advance. Preheat oven to 350°F. Butter and flour a bundt pan and set aside. In a large bowl, cream butter and sugar together until light and fluffy. Add eggs 2 at a time, beating well after each addition. Add vanilla and burnt sugar. In a separate bowl, sift together the remaining dry ingredients. Add slowly to the large bowl, mixing well. The batter will be very heavy. Add approximately 2 cups of the fruit mixture (or less according to taste). Mix well. Pour into well-greased and -floured cake pans. Bake at 350°F for about 1 hour or until a knife inserted in the middle comes out clean.

Once the cake is cooled (do not remove it from the tin), pour approximately ¼ cup of rum over it. Cover tightly with aluminum foil. Check the cake every 2 to 3 days. If it becomes dry, add some more rum. Continue in this manner for 1 month. (You might not have to add any rum to it after 2 weeks, but keep checking it.)

*Makes 8 servings.*

## FRUIT MIXTURE

**1 pound seeded dates, coarsely chopped**
**1 pound raisins, coarsely chopped**
**1 pound currants, coarsely chopped**
**1 pound cherries, coarsely chopped**

Approximately one month in advance of making the cake, place fruit in a jar that can be tightly sealed. Cover the fruit with rum, cover tightly, and store in a cool, dark place.

*Makes 4 pounds.*

# Index of Names

# Index of Recipes